Born and Bred?

Leade[illegible] [illegible]art and informal ed[illegible]

Michele Erina Doyle and
Mark K. Smith

For Chris Dunning and Charlie Harris.

Two men who bring heart to their work, recognize it in others, and foster it in the field.

Published by YMCA George Williams College for the Rank Foundation, 199 Freemasons Road, Canning Town, London E16 3PY

British Cataloguing in Publication Data
A catalogue record for this book is available from the British Library

Michele Erina Doyle and Mark K. Smith

Born and Bred? Leadership, heart and informal education

ISBN 1 870319 12 5

Typeset in Book Antiqua and Gill Sans
Cover: Spider
Printed by KLM

Contents

Exhibits

Introduction

> *I never really think of my work in terms of leadership. It's not a word I tend to associate with.*
>
> *I don't think it is necessary to develop people as leaders. I think that the term 'leadership' is not relevant and really not important. It immediately creates ... a dynamic that I think ... belongs in the past.*
>
> *Leaders are necessary, though I suppose I'd rather have the word facilitator than leader.*

Many informal educators, like these three, have a problem with 'leadership'. For some the word conjures up nasty images like the Pied Piper leading the children of Hamelin into oblivion. For others it may smack of elitism and privilege. Certain individuals seem destined to gain positions of power and influence. Born into the 'right' families, they go to 'right' schools and get the 'right' jobs. For them leadership may be viewed as a birthright, an inheritance that is developed through breeding. To this select group we may add those born with the 'right' qualities but with few of the privileges who, against the odds, work their way up the ladder.

We want to show that leadership isn't about the actions of a few privileged or 'gifted' individuals. It concerns all people and all situations. We experience and exercise it in just about every area of our lives. It is part of the routines of our homes and our daily contacts with others. In other words, we are all born to it. As one worker put it, 'Leadership to me is around taking some form of responsibility in any given situation.... Different people are leaders at different times'. Since leadership is part and parcel of our existence we need to come to some understanding of its nature and how it may work in practice.

There is more. To think of leadership as the qualities of a select group of people rather than as a process in which we are all involved, may be to walk away from our responsibilities as citizens. We can always look to others to do the work and take the blame. There are great dangers here. In times of uncertainty and change it is common to turn to people who can offer 'solutions', and who seem to have strength and vision. By doing this, we may escape some pain and anxiety. However, a desire for quick solutions can lead us to act in ways that demean and exploit others and ourselves. It can also make the problem worse or create more difficulties. By becoming too dependent on leaders and their vision, we fail to involve ourselves in making solutions. Many of the issues that affect our lives – around, for example, the environment, poverty, racism – can only be properly addressed if we are all involved in facing up to hard questions.

Leadership, for us then, is not about influencing groups and communities to follow a particular person's vision, but rather working so that people may come together, flourish and build better lives. It is something that grows and may be cultivated (bred). We believe there is a need to move beyond a focus on the leader as a particular kind of person, into a view of leadership as a shared process. In part one of *Born and Bred?* we start to make the case for judging leadership in terms of the contribution made to the happiness of all.

Our concern is to cultivate leadership with heart. It is a leadership with a passion for service, association and flourishing. It calls upon us to respond with our spirit, conscience and the core of our being. In part two of the book we begin to explore what all this might mean for leadership and for ourselves. Having looked at the hope leadership holds for all of us we then move on to examine the contribution of informal education.

How are we to develop and sustain leadership with heart? This book has been written in the belief that informal educators like youth, community, and community education workers have a special role to play. A significant number have contributed in various ways to this book (see page 5). Their concern with conversation and relationships is of fundamental importance. What is more, the groups and organizations they work with and in, are environments where leadership with heart can flourish.[1] They can involve service, association and a care for wellbeing. In part three we focus on informal educators as animators, educators and formators (trainers). We offer guidance as to how informal educators can work so that leadership with heart is born and bred in practice.

Linked resources

This publication links with a number of other resources:

- *The Born and Bred? CD* created by Peter Cutts, is a mosaic of pieces that explore some experiences of leadership and work with young people in agencies funded by the Rank Charities.

- *The Born and Bred? web pages* has material on the agencies featured in the CD, links and activities associated with each of the chapters in this book, and examples of further resources and activities. The web site can be found at www.infed.org/bornandbred.

- *The Born and Bred? Resource Pack* is a printed version of a selection of the material available on the web.

- *Informal Education: conversation, democracy and learning.* This sister book and associated web pages (at www.infed.org/foundations), provide a further exploration of some of the ideas and practices mentioned in this text.

---

[1] This point is developed by Tony Jeffs and Mark K. Smith in (1999) *Informal Education: conversation, democracy and learning* 2e, Ticknall: Education Now.

Quotes

All the quotations printed in italic are taken from interviews with informal educators - youth workers, community educators and housing workers. Some of the interviews form part of the *Born and Bred?* CD created by Peter Cutts. A further eight workers were interviewed by Huw Blacker in March and April 1999.

Acknowledgements

Our thanks to Huw Blacker and to Peter Cutts for all their work. Thanks also to the following people who agreed to be interviewed: Nash Ali, Joanne Bartlett, Greg Barton, Julie Benson, Rachel Davies, David Davoll, Melissa Desbonnes, Kate Doherty, Mike Gilesenan, Robert James, Millie Lewis, Anita McDade, Janine Mahagan, Erica Meyerick, David Petrie, Richard Pitt, Christopher Richards, Tina Smith, Pip Wilson and all at the Magnet Young Adult Centre and the Newry and Mourne Arts Collective.

We also need to thank Kate Bennett, Dave Coates, Eileen Doyle, Chris Dunning, Richard Jones, Charlie Harris, Marilyn Iwanuschuk, John McCormack, Rachel MacDonald, Una Murray, and Lynne Thomas for their assistance in putting the book and other resources together. A special thanks, also, to Mary Crosby, Tony Jeffs and Mary Wolfe for their critical eye.

Our son Michael Harry was carried and born whilst writing this book and it would not be complete without mentioning him.

Part one

Leadership

In this part of *Born and Bred?* we explore leadership. We look first at what we have called 'classical leadership'. This pictures leaders as people who have special qualities. They may also hold a position in a group or organization that allows them to direct others. Our second picture is of leadership as a social process - something that goes on all the time in relationships and groups.

We argue that leadership involves making judgements about what is good and evil. In other words, for something to be called 'leadership' it must add to human happiness. From there we look at what inclusive forms of leadership involve. We have called this approach 'shared leadership' because of its concern for interaction, and with building communities and ways of living where all may share in a common life.

Chapter one

Classical leadership

> *I think there are particular people that others will follow, for whatever reason. Perhaps they have a sense of humour, they like their style.*

> *When you look at organising events it's somebody who's got what is termed as 'leadership qualities', they are people who are willing to tell other people what to do but have the respect of other people as well, or gain that respect.*

Many of the images associated with leadership have their roots in conflict. It is the stuff of generals who outwit their opponents, politicians who convince and channel groups into action, and people who take control of a crisis. We are directed to special individuals like Gandhi or Joan of Arc; Napoleon or Hitler. The stories around such people seem to show that there are moments of crisis or decision where the actions of one person are pivotal. They have a vision of what can, and should be, done and can communicate this to others. When these are absent there can be trouble. Quality of leadership is, arguably, central to the survival and success of groups and organizations. As *The Art of War*, the oldest known military text (circa 400 BC), puts it, 'the leader of armies is the arbiter of the people's fate, the man on whom it depends whether the nation shall be in peace or in peril'.[2]

---

[2] Sun Tzu, Waging war (20) in *The Art of War*, http://kappeli.ton.tut.fi/aow/main.html

But what is leadership? It seems to be one of those qualities that you know when you see it, but is difficult to describe. There are almost as many definitions as there are commentators. Many associate leadership with one person leading. Four things stand out in this respect. First, to lead involves influencing others. Second, where there are leaders there are followers. Third, leaders seem to come to the fore when there is a crisis or special problem. In other words, they often become visible when an innovative response is needed. Fourth, leaders are people who have a clear idea of what they want to achieve and why. Thus, leaders are people who are able to think and act creatively in non-routine situations – and who set out to influence the actions, beliefs and feelings of others. In this sense being a 'leader' is personal. It flows from an individual's qualities and actions. However, it is also often linked to some other role such as manager or expert. Here there can be a lot of confusion. Not all managers, for example, are leaders; and not all leaders are managers.

Traits

Leaders are people, who are able to express themselves fully, says Warren Bennis. 'They also know what they want', he continues, 'why they want it, and how to communicate what they want to others, in order to gain their co-operation and support.' Lastly, 'they know how to achieve their goals'.[3] But what is it that makes someone exceptional in this respect? As soon as we study the lives of people who have been labelled as great or effective leaders, it becomes clear that they have very different qualities. We only have to think of political figures like Nelson Mandela, Margaret Thatcher and Mao Zedong to confirm this.

Instead of starting with exceptional individuals many turned to setting out the general qualities or *traits* they believed should be present. Pick up almost any of the popular books on the subject and you will find a list of traits

---

[3] Walter Bennis (1998) *On Becoming a Leader*, London: Arrow. See page 3.

that are thought to be central to effective leadership. The basic idea is that if a person possesses these she or he will be able to take the lead in very different situations. At first glance, the lists seem to be helpful (see, for example, *Exhibit 1*). But spend any time around them and they can leave a lot to be desired.

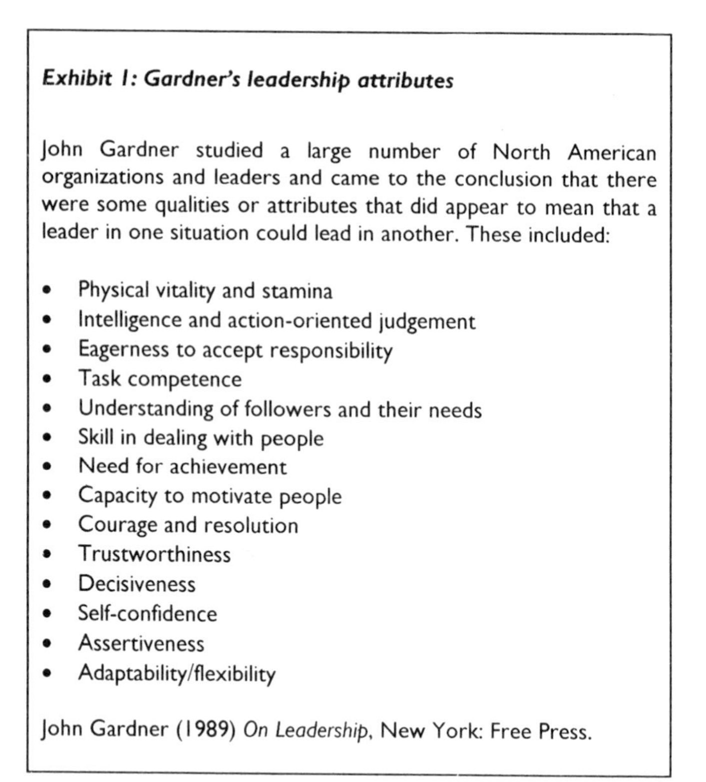

Exhibit 1: Gardner's leadership attributes

John Gardner studied a large number of North American organizations and leaders and came to the conclusion that there were some qualities or attributes that did appear to mean that a leader in one situation could lead in another. These included:

- Physical vitality and stamina
- Intelligence and action-oriented judgement
- Eagerness to accept responsibility
- Task competence
- Understanding of followers and their needs
- Skill in dealing with people
- Need for achievement
- Capacity to motivate people
- Courage and resolution
- Trustworthiness
- Decisiveness
- Self-confidence
- Assertiveness
- Adaptability/flexibility

John Gardner (1989) *On Leadership*, New York: Free Press.

The first problem is that the early searchers after traits often assumed that there was a definite set of characteristics that made a leader - whatever the situation. In other words, they thought the same traits would work on a battlefield and in the staff room of a school. They minimized the impact of the situation. They, and later writers, also tended to mix some very different qualities. Some of Gardner's qualities, for example, are aspects of a person's behaviour, some are skills, and others are to do with temperament and intellectual ability. Like other lists of this nature it is quite long - so what happens when someone has some but not all of the qualities? On the other hand, the list is not exhaustive and it is possible that someone might have other 'leadership qualities'. What of these?

More recently people have tried looking at what combinations of traits might be good for a particular situation. There is some mileage in this. It appears possible to link clusters of personality traits to success in different situations. But it remains an inexact science!

One of the questions we hear most often around such lists concerns their apparent 'maleness'. When men and women are asked about each other's characteristics and leadership qualities, some significant patterns emerge. Both tend to have difficulties in seeing women as leaders. The attributes associated with leadership on these lists are often viewed as male. However, whether the characteristics of leaders can be gendered is questionable. If it is next to impossible to make a list of leadership traits that stands up to questioning, then the same certainly applies to lists of gender specific leadership traits!

Behaviours

As the early researchers ran out of steam in their search for traits, they turned to what leaders did - how they behaved (especially towards followers). They moved from leaders to leadership. Different patterns of behaviour were grouped together and labelled as styles. This became a very popular activity within management training. Various schemes appeared, designed to diagnose and develop people's style of working. Despite different names, the basic ideas were very similar. The four main styles that appear are:

- **Concern for task**. Here leaders emphasize the achievement of concrete objectives. They look for high levels of productivity, and ways to organize people and activities in order to meet those objectives.

- **Concern for people**. In this style, leaders look upon their followers as people - their needs, interests, problems, development and so on. They are not simply units of production or means to an end.

- **Directive leadership**. This style is characterized by leaders taking decisions for others - and expecting followers or subordinates to follow instructions.
- **Participative leadership**. Here leaders try to share decision-making with others. [4]

Often, we find two of these styles present in books and training materials. For example, concern for task is set against concern for people; and directive is contrasted with participative leadership. If you have been on a teamwork or leadership development course then it is likely you will have come across some variant of this in an exercise or discussion.

Many of the early writers looked to participative and people-centred leadership, arguing that it brought about greater satisfaction amongst followers (subordinates). However, when the researchers really got to work on this it didn't seem to stand up. There were lots of differences between studies. It was difficult to say style of leadership was significant in enabling one group to work better than another. Perhaps the main problem, though, was one shared with those who looked for traits. The researchers did not look properly at the context or setting in which the style was used. Is it possible that the same style would work as well in a gang or group of friends, and in a hospital emergency room? The styles that leaders can adopt are far more affected by those they are working with, and the environment they are operating within, than had been originally thought.

Situations

Researchers began to turn to the contexts in which leadership is exercised - and the idea that what is needed changes from situation to situation. Some looked to the processes by which leaders emerge in different circumstances - for example at moments of great crisis or where there is a vacuum. Others turned to the ways in which leaders and followers viewed each other in various contexts

---

[4] Sumarized by Peter Wright (1996) in *Managerial Leadership*, London: Routledge, pages 36-7.

- for example in the army, political parties and in companies. The most extreme view was that just about everything was determined by the context. But most writers did not take this route. They brought the idea of style with them, believing that the style needed would change with the situation. Another way of putting this is that particular contexts would demand particular forms of leadership. This placed a premium on people who were able to develop an ability to work in different ways, and could change their style to suit the situation.

What began to develop was a *contingency* approach. The central idea was that effective leadership was dependent on a mix of factors. For example, Fred E. Fielder argued that effectiveness depends on two interacting factors: leadership style and the degree to which the situation gives the leader control and influence. Three things are important here:

- **The relationship between the leaders and followers**. If leaders are liked and respected they are more likely to have the support of others.
- **The structure of the task**. If the task is clearly spelled out as to goals, methods and standards of performance then it is more likely that leaders will be able to exert influence.
- **Position power**. If an organization or group confers powers on the leader for the purpose of getting the job done, then this may well increase the influence of the leader.[5]

Models like this can help us to think about what we are doing in different situations. For example, we may be more directive where a quick response is needed, and where people are used to being told what to do, rather than having to work at it themselves.

However, aside from their very general nature, there are some issues with such models. First, much that has been

---

[5] Fred E. Fieldler and Joseph E. Garcia (1987) *New Approaches to Effective Leadership,* New York: John Wiley. These qualities are discussed on pages 51 - 67.

written has a North American bias. There is a lot of evidence to suggest cultural factors influence the way that people carry out, and respond to, different leadership styles. For example, some cultures are more individualistic, or value family as against bureaucratic models, or have very different expectations about how people address and talk with each other. All this impacts on the choice of style and approach.

Second, as we saw earlier, there may be different patterns of leadership linked with men and women. Some have argued that women may have leadership styles that are more nurturing, caring and sensitive. They look more to relationships. Men are said to look to task. However, there is a lot of debate about this. We can find plenty of examples of nurturing men and task-oriented women. Any contrasts between the style of men and women may be down to the situation. In management, for example, women are more likely to be in positions of authority in people-oriented sectors – so this aspect of style is likely to be emphasized.

Authority

Frequently we confuse leadership with authority. [6] Authority is often seen as the possession of powers based on formal role. In organizations, for example, we tend to focus on the manager or officer. They are seen as people who have the right to direct us. We obey them because we see their exercise of power as legitimate. It may also be that we fear the consequences of not following their orders or 'requests'. The possibility of them sacking, demoting or disadvantaging us may well secure our compliance. We may also follow them because they show leadership. As we have seen, the latter is generally something more informal - the ability to make sense of, and act in, situations that are out of the ordinary. In this way, leaders don't simply influence; they have to show that crises or unexpected events and experiences do not faze them. Leaders may have formal

---

[6] This is discussed in Ronald A. Heifetz (1994) *Leadership Without Easy Answers*, Cambridge, MA: Belknap Press. What follows is also based on Heifetz.

authority, but they rely in large part on informal authority. This flows from their personal qualities and actions. They may be trusted, respected for their expertise, or followed because of their ability to persuade.

Leaders have authority as part of an exchange: if they fail to deliver the goods, to meet people's expectations, they run the risk of authority being removed and given to another. Those who have formal authority over them may take this action. However, we also need to consider the other side. Followers, knowingly or unknowingly, accept the right of the person to lead - and he or she is dependent on this. The leader also relies on 'followers' for feedback and contributions. Without these they will not have the information and resources to do their job. Leaders and followers are interdependent.

People who do not have formal positions of power can also enjoy informal authority. In a football team, for example, the manager may not be the most influential person. It could be an established player who can read the game and energise that colleagues turn to. In politics a classic example is Gandhi - who for much of the time held no relevant formal position - but through his example and his thinking became an inspiration for others.

Having formal authority is both a resource and a constraint. On the one hand it can bring access to systems and resources. Handled well it can help people feel safe. On the other hand, formal authority carries a set of expectations - and these can be quite unrealistic in times of crisis. As Heifetz puts it, 'raise hard questions and one risks getting cut down, even if the questions are important for moving forward on the problem'.[7] Being outside the formal power structure, but within an organization, can be an advantage. You can have more freedom of movement, the chance of focussing on what you see as the issue (rather than the organization's focus), and there is a stronger chance of being in touch with what people are feeling 'at the frontline'.

---

[7] Heifetz (1994) page 180. The advantages of being outside formal authority structures are summarized on page 188.

Charisma

Before moving on it is important to look at the question of charisma. It is so much a part of how we look at leadership - but is such a difficult quality to tie down. Charisma is, literally, a gift of grace or of God. Max Weber, more than anyone, brought this idea into the realm of leadership. He used 'charisma' to talk about self-appointed leaders who are followed by those in distress. Such leaders gain influence because they are seen as having special talents or gifts that can help people escape the pain they are in.[8]

When thinking about charisma we often look to the qualities of particular individuals - their skills, personality and presence. But this is only one side of things. We need to explore the situations in which charisma arises. When strong feelings of distress are around there does seem to be a tendency to turn to figures who seem to have answers. To make our lives easier we may want to put the burden of finding and making solutions on someone else. In this way we help to make the role for 'charismatic leaders' to step into. They in turn will seek to convince us of their special gifts and of their solution to the crisis or problem. When these things come together something very powerful can happen. It doesn't necessarily mean that the problem is dealt with - but we can come to believe it is. Regarding such leaders with awe, perhaps being inspired in different ways by them, we can begin to feel safer and directed. This can be a great resource. Someone like Martin Luther King used the belief that people had in him to take forward civil rights in the United States. He was able to contain a lot of the stress his supporters felt and give hope of renewal. He articulated a vision of what was possible and worked with people to develop strategies. But there are also considerable dangers.

Charisma involves dependency. It can mean giving up our responsibilities. Sadly, it is all too easy to let others who seem to know what they are doing get on with difficult

---

[8] Gerth, H. H. and Mills, C. Wright (eds.) (1991) *From Max Weber. Essays in Sociology*, London: Routledge, pages 51 - 55.

matters. By placing people on a pedestal the distance between 'us' and 'them' widens. They seem so much more able or in control. Rather than facing up to situations, and making our own solutions, we remain followers (and are often encouraged to do so). There may well come a point when the lie implicit in this confronts us. Just as we turned to charismatic leaders, we can turn against them. It could be we recognize that the 'solution' we signed up to has not made things better. It might be that some scandal or incident reveals the leader in what we see as a bad light. Whatever, we can end up blaming, and even destroying, the leader. Unfortunately, we may simply turn to another rather than looking to our own capacities.

In conclusion

In this chapter we have tried to set out some of the elements of a 'classical' view of leadership. We have seen how commentators have searched for special traits and behaviours and looked at the different situations where leaders work and emerge. Running through much of this is a set of beliefs that we can describe as a classical view of leadership where leaders:

- Tend to be identified by position. They are part of the hierarchy.
- Become the focus for answers and solutions. We look to them when we don't know what to do, or when we can't be bothered to work things out for ourselves.
- Give direction and have vision.
- Have special qualities setting them apart. These help to create the gap between leaders and followers.

This view of leadership sits quite comfortably with the forms of organization that are common in business, the armed forces and government. Where the desire is to get something done, to achieve a narrow range of objectives in a short period of time, then it may make sense to think in this way. However, this has its dangers. Whilst some 'classical' leaders may have a more participative style, it is still just a style. A great deal of power remains in their hands and the opportunity for all to take responsibility and face larger questions is curtailed. It can also feed into a 'great-man' model of leadership and minimize our readiness to question those who present us with easy answers. As our awareness of our own place in the making of leadership grows, we may be less ready to hand our responsibilities to others. We may also come to realize our own power:

> *I don't think it's actually possible to lead somebody. I think you can allow yourself to be led. It's a bit like other things - you can't teach, you can only learn - because you can only control yourself.*

More inclusive and informal understandings of leadership offer some interesting possibilities, as we will see in the next chapter.

Follow up

There are several things you can do to follow up the exploration of leadership in this chapter.

Born and Bred? CD: Listen to David Davoll talk about bringing leadership to the surface - *In the dock* (track one).

Born and Bred? web pages: Visit the classical leadership page at www.infed.org/bornandbred. You'll find extra activities, further reading and links to related pages.

Chapter two

Shared leadership

The group took over. There was a whole group leadership thing. I don't think leadership's necessarily about one person sometimes - everyone has the qualities of being a leader or taking some form of responsibility in their lives, and sometimes that's a whole group ethos.

I want to work in a situation where people can take on roles and responsibilities, tasks, whatever they want to do. As long as I can assist in this, rather than being the forerunning force taking it over, then that's what I'm aiming for.

Leadership can be explored as a social process - something that happens between people. It is not so much what leaders do, as something that arises out of social relationships. As such it does not depend on one person, but on how people act together to make sense of the situations that face them. It is happening all the time.

Everyday leadership

If we look at everyday life - the situations and groups we are involved in - then we soon find leadership. Friends deciding how they are going to spend an evening, families negotiating over housework - each involve influence and decision. However, such leadership often does not reside in a person. It may be shared and can move. In one situation an individual may be influential because of their expertise or position, in another it can be someone completely different. What these people may be able to do is to offer an idea or an action that helps to focus or restructure the situation - and the way in which others see things.

Sometimes there may not even be one person we can readily label as leader - just a group working together to achieve what is wanted. Rather than people leading, it is ideals and ideas. We don't follow an individual; we follow the conversation. Through listening and contributing, thoughts and feelings emerge and develop. It is not the force of personality that leads us on, but the rightness of what is said. Other factors may also operate.

From this we can see that it is not our position that is necessarily important, but our behaviour. The question is whether or not our actions help groups and relationships to work and achieve. Actions that do this could be called leadership - and can come from any group member. Many writers - especially those looking at management - tend to talk about leadership as a person having a clear vision and the ability to make it real. However, as we have begun to discover, leadership lies not so much in one person having a clear vision as in our capacity to work with others in creating one.

We may also recognize the power of self-leadership, as one worker put it: 'me trying to get the most out of my own resources'. Some people have talked of this as the influence we exert on ourselves 'to achieve the self-motivation and self-direction we need to perform'.[9] Such self-motivation and self-direction can impact on others. The worker continued:

> *[It] then moves onto staff, for them to discover the self-resources that they have within themselves and then look for anything that needs developing... For young people, it's about getting them to realise their self-leadership, to realise their own potential.*

The leadership process is part of our daily experience. We may lead others, ourselves, or be led. We play our part

---

[9] Charles C. Manz and Henry P. Sims Jr. (1989) *Superleadership: Leading others to lead themselves*, New York: Prentice Hall.

in relationships and groups where it is always around. Sometimes there is an obvious 'leader', often there isn't. Nor are there always obvious followers. The world is not neatly divided in this respect. Part of our responsibility as partners in the process is to work so that those who may label themselves as followers come to see that they, too, are leaders.

> *What I understand of leadership is encouraging, or getting, people to realise their own resources, what they've got within them.*

As individuals we are part of the leadership process and, at times, receive the gift of being the leader from others.

Ethics

We also want to take things a stage further. For something to qualify as 'leadership' we must also make judgements about the quality of what happens. It should enrich the lives we all lead. Here we want to highlight two aspects. Leadership must be:

- **Inclusive** – we all share in the process.
- **Elevating** - we become wiser and better people by being involved.

We want to include these ethical qualities so that we can make proper judgements about leadership. For example, if we stay with a simple, technical definition then we can look at a figure like Hitler and say he was, in many respects, a great leader. He had a vision, was able to energize a large number of people around it, and develop the effectiveness of the organizations he was responsible for. However, as soon as we ask whether his actions were inclusive and elevating we come to a very different judgement. He was partly responsible for the death and exclusion of millions of people. He focused people's attention on the actions of external enemies, internal scapegoats and false images of community while avoiding facing a deeper analysis of the country's ills.

> Hitler wielded power, but he did not lead. He played to people's basest needs and fears. If he inspired people toward the common good of Germany, it was

> the good of a truncated and exclusive society feeding off others.[10]

We could go on. Hitler's failings weren't just moral. Hopefully, the point is made. Leadership involves making ethical as well as technical judgements.

Aspects of the approach we are exploring here are sometimes called democratic leadership. It involves people, and can foster a belief in democratic principles and processes such as self-determination and participation. These are concerns that we share. However, we want to widen things out. We want to include everyday behaviour that is inclusive and looks to enriching all our lives, but that does not have an explicit democratic focus. We call this 'shared leadership'.

For such leadership to develop we need to pay special attention to three things. We need to encourage:

- **Ownership**. Problems and issues need to become a responsibility of all with proper chances for people to share and participate.
- **Learning**. An emphasis on learning and development is necessary so that people can share, understand and contribute to what's going on.
- **Sharing**. Open, respectful and informed conversation is central.[11]

We want to look at each of these in turn.

Ownership

> *Leadership to me is around taking some form of responsibility in any given situation*

[10] Ronald A. Heifetz (1994), page 24.

[11] These are developments of areas suggested by John Gastil (1997) 'A definition and illustration of democratic leadership' in Keith Grint (ed.) *Leadership*, Oxford: Oxford University Press.

There are some very practical reasons for encouraging people to own the problems facing them. For example, where the problem is non-routine and needs an unusual response, it is important to have the right information. Involving those with a stake in the situation - especially those at the sharp end - gives a chance for insights to emerge. Further, the more people take on an issue or problem as theirs, and involve themselves in thinking through responses, the more likely they are to act and to carry things through. They have an investment in making things happen. It is their solution, not somebody else's. In a lot of situations we may simply comply with what our manager, parent or friend tells us to do. It saves us thinking. More importantly it allows us to blame them if things go wrong. Sometimes we just 'buy-in' to a suggestion - we can see the sense of it, but don't commit to it. As a result, we are less likely to stick with it when the going gets tough. We can also still blame the suggestion-maker in some way - 'I wish I'd never listened to you'. When we own a problem it becomes our responsibility. If things go wrong when trying to find a solution, we cannot blame others. For these reasons alone we may be very resistant to shouldering responsibility.

We may also be frightened and lost. Sometimes the issue facing us is so complex or of such a scale that we don't know where to start. We may be worried about getting things wrong, of not understanding what the issues are, or adding to conflict. Faced by a crisis or an apparently insoluble problem, we may look for strong leadership. It may be through anxiety, hostility or helplessness (to name just a few emotions) that we are ready to turn to those who seem to have an answer. There is a triple danger here. First, these powerful emotions may well push us to project all sorts of capacities onto the 'leader' that she or he does not possess. Because they talk a good talk, or look the part, we may want to believe that they know what they are doing and have our interests at heart. Second, the desire to rid ourselves of uncertainties and worries can lead us to turn away from our responsibilities. It is so much easier if someone else can take on the worries. Third, we can overlook the extent to which we contribute to the situation. It may be our actions, or our opinions that are helping to make the crisis.

The issue here is how we contain our distress enough to get over any initial hurdles. We need a breathing space. With friends, families and work colleagues we often turn to 'a safe pair of hands' to achieve this. Safety here is less about being told what to do, as feeling that we have some sort of structure supporting or maintaining us. We need a holding environment in which our attentions are focused and we can begin to work on the problem. Within a community group, for example, there may well be someone who is able to say something like, 'I don't have the answers, but if we take things bit by bit, we may find a way through'. This is a classic way of holding the situation. Actions such as breaking things into smaller pieces and trying to slow the pace down a little help us to put our brains into gear and to put panic to one side.

We may also try to avoid taking responsibility for things because we are lazy or want others to do things for us. After all, if we own a problem then we will have to act at some point. Why bother exerting ourselves if we can sit back and let someone else take the strain? This takes us straight into the realm of ethical questions. Is it fair that someone should take a ride on the back of others? Is it right to benefit from belonging to a group or community without making the fullest contribution we can?

Learning

> *I don't think leadership is about being a manager and cracking the whip and getting people to do the job, but do I think it is about just keeping the learning on track, so there is some sort of agreed... way forward.*

To act for the best we need to be informed. Our actions have to be shaped by a good understanding of the situation and of the possibilities open to us. We also need to develop some very practical skills and to attend to our feelings. In short we need to deepen our understanding, develop, and share in this with others. Leadership entails learning. It means becoming wiser and more knowledgeable.

Wisdom is not something that we possess like a book or computer. It is a quality that appears in action. The people we describe as wise do not necessarily know a lot of things.

They are not encyclopaedias. Rather, they are able to reflect on a situation and, as likely or not, encourage others to join with them. Crucially they are also able to relate this to the sorts of practical actions that are right for the situation. In other words, wisdom is concerned with making choices about something that has to be done or not done. And to act wisely we must think and evaluate. This is more than cleverness. We must want, and be able, to make some sense of what life throws at us. Knowing about lots of different things is of little use if that knowledge cannot be related to the problem that is facing us at this moment.

Yet there is something more at work here. Wisdom is wrapped up with morality. To be wise, we would argue, is also to have a care for people (including ourselves) and for how we may all live more fulfilling lives. If we are to think and to evaluate we must have standards by which to judge what we find. This means looking to what philosophers like Aristotle talked about as the good life. This involves having an understanding of the different things that need to come together if people are to flourish. There will be countless arguments about what this actually entails. People have different experiences of life and, as a result, see the world in contrary ways. Knowing this we should be ready to explore beliefs, hopes and feelings with each other. There is no monopoly on truth - but we do need to take a position. To act we must come to some decisions about what may help us to live fulfilled lives e.g. having food in our stomachs, a roof over our heads, a chance to contribute to society and so on. Some people argue that there is a hierarchy of needs around such matters - that we need to eat and have shelter before we look to other areas of fulfilment. Others disagree. Wisdom lies in not having fixed ideas here, but in taking a position and modifying it in the light of experience. We must have some humility - to be open to others, to experiences and to criticism.

This is a theme picked up by writers like Ronald A. Heifetz. He argues that true leaders are educators. Their task is to work with communities to face problems and lead themselves rather than to influence people to agree to a particular position. They help to build environments in which people can reflect upon how they can help with solving problems and with achieving goals. Furthermore, we can add, there is a need to develop people's ability to make decisions, work together and think in ways that respect others.

Sharing

> *I feel if there's openness and honest sharing, I think you can deal with (things). If the climate is not set, people won't share and (things) are harder to deal with.*

Alongside spreading ownership and cultivating learning we need to develop open and productive ways of sharing our thoughts and feelings. This isn't just so that we can make better decisions, but also so we can talk and be with others. Through this we may learn about them, ourselves, and find our place in the world. In short, this means developing conversations that involve people, deepen understanding and help us make sound judgements and decisions.

Good conversation involves us in co-operating, thinking of each other's feelings and experiences, and giving each room to talk. The virtues it involves are central to building stronger and healthier communities:

- **Concern**. To be with people, engaging them in conversation involves commitment to each other. We feel something for the other person as well as the topic.
- **Trust.** We have to take what others are saying in good faith. This is not the same as being gullible. While we may take things on trust, we will be looking to check whether our trust is being abused.
- **Respect**. While there may be large differences between partners in conversation, the process can only go on if there is mutual regard.
- **Appreciation**. Linked to respect, this involves valuing the unique qualities that others bring.
- **Affection**. Conversation involves a feeling with, and for, those taking part.

- **Hope**. We engage in conversation in the belief that it holds possibility. Often it is not clear what we will gain or learn, but faith in the process carries us forward. [12]

In good conversation the topic takes over. It leads us, rather than us leading it. Sometimes we may interpret this as the speaker leading the group.

> *I think if you're discussing or conversing with a group, when anybody talks I suppose they lead the conversation in a certain direction, therefore, however short or long it may be, they're taking a leadership role in that group.*

One way of trying to work out whether it is a particular person leading, or if the conversation itself has taken over, is to think about people's frame of mind. For example, are they going into a conversation thinking they are right? If we are trying to win the argument or score points then we are less likely to hear the truth in what others are saying. Playing that sort of game can result in everyone losing out. Conversation flows. It takes on different shapes and forms. If we keep hitting the same line then knowledge doesn't deepen; wisdom doesn't grow. Where conversation has taken over, people run with the exchanges and gain learning from that. It turns into a journey of discovery rather than a route with a fixed destination. For leadership this can be liberating. It means that as individuals we don't have to know the answers. What we need is to develop ways of being in conversation (including silence) that allow those answers to surface.

How do we do this? We deliberate. This entails weighing up situations and coming to an understanding. Crucially, it also involves coming to decisions. This requires:

- Constructive participation.
- Facilitation.
- The maintenance of healthy relationships.

---

[12] Nicholas C. Burbules (1993) *Dialogue in Teaching*, New York: Teachers College Press.

- A positive emotional setting.[13]

People need to be involved in ways that allow them to face-up to situations and take responsibility. Often there will be times when individuals and groups require help to work together. Such facilitation may come from people within a group (and we may label it as leadership), or it may come from someone like an informal educator. Relationships, and how people feel about each other, often get in the way. Here 'leaders' or facilitators take on a special role. They can help people to shift from a focus on the topic to the processes they are going through and the feelings involved (and vice versa). All this can help build an environment in which there is respect and sharing.

Uncovering what it is that people want to talk about, defining issues, weighing up alternatives and making decisions on ways forward are not easy. They do not happen in some simple step-by-step fashion. There is ebb and flow. Rushing towards a decision might bring some sense of achievement but can crowd out the richness of dialogue. Going with the flow can allow people the space and time to make wise choices. Balance this with a concern for focus, relationships and feelings, and the virtues of conversation, and we open up a space where wisdom can flourish.

In conclusion

In this and the last chapter we have seen some deeply contrasting views of leadership. There are various ways of talking about these, but we thought the most helpful for the moment was to compare classical and shared leadership (see *Exhibit 2*).

Presented like this we can see how easy it is for people to misunderstand each other. When we talk of leadership are we looking to position or process, individual activity or social interaction, orders or conversation? What one person means can be very different to another. It is also clear why many informal educators like youth workers are unhappy

---

[13] These headings come from John Gastil (1997) pp.161-163.

talking of leadership. Their understanding often leans to the classical. If it were the other way it might be a very different picture. 'Shared leadership' carries some familiar qualities for informal educators.

Exhibit 2: Classical and shared leadership compared

Classical leadership	*Shared leadership*
Displayed by a person's position in a group or hierarchy.	Identified by the quality of people's interactions rather than their position.
Leadership evaluated by whether the leader solves problems.	Leadership evaluated by how people are working together.
Leaders provide solutions and answers.	All work to enhance the process and to make it more fulfilling.
Distinct differences between leaders and followers: character, skill, etc.	People are interdependent. All are active participants in the process of leadership.
Communication is often formal.	Communication is crucial with a stress on conversation.
Can often rely on secrecy, deception and payoffs.	Values democratic processes, honesty and shared ethics. Seeks a common good.

Drawing from material in Gloria Nemerowicz and Eugene Rosi (1997) *Education for Leadership and Social Responsibility*, London: Falmer Press. Page 16.

Both approaches have their pitfalls. We have already discussed some of the problems with classical approaches. Here we highlight four associated with shared leadership. First, the emphasis on process can lead to a lack of attention to product or outcome. It can provide an alibi for laziness and incompetence when little is achieved. Care needs to be taken not to lose sight of the question or problem that is the subject of decision-making. Second, the emphasis on group life within shared leadership approaches may mean that the excellence or flair of the individual is not rewarded. The person concerned can experience this as unfair and demotivating - and the group may lose out as a result. Resentment might grow, and innovative solutions to problems may not be forthcoming. There will be times when it makes sense to follow the lead of a gifted individual. Third, the commitments, understandings and practices of shared leadership are sophisticated and it is easy to see why, at this level alone, people may shy away from it. It is an 'ideal model' and, as such, can easily mutate. Fourth, all models of leadership are culturally specific. What may be viewed as appropriate in one society or group may not be so in another.

This said, thinking about leadership in these ways allows us to begin to get to the heart of what it may involve - and how we and informal educators like youth workers, community workers and those concerned with lifelong learning may respond (see Chapter 6).

Follow up

There are several things you can do to follow up the exploration of leadership in this chapter.

Born and Bred? CD: Listen to the people involved with the Magnet Centre on *All together now* (track 5).

Born and Bred? web pages: Visit the shared leadership page at www.infed.org/bornandbred. You'll find extra activities, further reading, and links to related pages.

Part two

Heart and leadership

Leadership is not just some technical process. It is a very human activity. In part two of *Born and Bred?* we suggest that if it is to be inclusive and elevating it needs a 'heart'. This involves us in exploring the kind of person we are, or wish to be; our moral sense or conscience; and our spirit. These qualities, which are often spoken of, but rarely addressed with regard to leadership, are the focus of chapter three.

From there we turn in chapter four to how leadership with heart may be expressed. In other words, what form might it take? We identify three aspects. First, it entails putting service to others over self-interest. Second, leadership with heart looks to association – the life of groups. Third, it means making a commitment to work for the well-being of all. We explore what each of these involves and some of the practical implications of choosing this path.

Chapter three

Heart

Having that knowledge with the heart, and that passion for football, which also helped. Knowing that I wanted to make a difference, that I wasn't just going to stand by and see all this suffering, all the negativity, and not do nothing about it, I wanted to try and change it. All I can do is try and I went with it.

In the previous chapters we have explored some theories around leadership. We have argued that we should judge it by its ability to enrich all our lives. We might describe this as leadership with heart. But what do we mean by this? Perhaps we ought to start with 'heart'.

Physiologically the heart is the internal organ that pumps blood around the body. However, it has come to mean so much more than that. We only have to think of the many sayings that use the word to see this. People may talk of having a heart to heart; of someone with their heart in the right place; of a person whose heart is broken; or of learning by heart. The list goes on, and no wonder. The heart is central to the body; it is at the core of things. It supports life; it is vital. With these properties it is easy to see why the word has become rich with meaning.

Here we want to explore three linked dimensions that we think capture something of what is involved when talking of leadership with heart. These are:

- **Spirit** – the passions that animate or move us.

- **Moral sense or conscience** – the values, ideals and attitudes that guide us.
- **Being** – the kind of person we are, or wish to be, in the world.

Spirit

In general we come to know and describe the world through our senses. We might experience the sight of Tower Bridge, the scent of roses, the taste of a chilli pepper, and so on. Sometimes moments after these experiences, we can describe them. For example, on tasting a chilli pepper we might exclaim 'that's hot'. We may also find that others have a similar experience. They might add to, or qualify, our description, 'too hot for me!' or 'it's not *that* hot'. Sometimes we can find agreement – chilli peppers are hot!

At times we come across things that are difficult to describe because they seem beyond our senses. Our experience of spirit is like that; hard to fathom. We may stumble with our words and agreement may be more difficult to find. How might we describe the experience? What is spirit? The word is used to describe a number of things from alcohol to God.

Our focus here is on the spirit of our actions and words; the motivation for what we say and do. In thinking about this, one writer posed the following question:

> Suppose that I ask myself, 'When I offered my seat to the old man on the subway train did I do this *in the right spirit*?' Such a question is an invitation to examine my motivation: 'Was I being genuinely altruistic or was I showing off to my companion, or even to myself?'[14]

---

[14] D. Evans (1993) *Spirituality and Human Nature*, New York: SUNY Press. This approach to spirit and spirituality is discussed by Alex Rodger (1996) 'Human spirituality: toward an educational rationale' in Ron Best (ed.) *Education, Spirituality and the Whole Child*, London: Cassell.

Alex Rodger comments that if we reflect on this question, we can see that a motive is literally something that we are *moved by*. The next question is, 'What moves us?' It is the feelings, ideas and relationships that we believe in, and commit to. The nature of these tells us much about our disposition - the kind of person we are in the world. For example, we might see a homeless person on the street. As a result, we may be moved to act in some way. We may give them money, write to our MP or donate something to a charity. Whatever our action, something is moving us. We can ask 'Do we feel guilty, angry, a sense of injustice?' Examining our answers gives some indication of the kind of person we are. We may describe ourselves as being kindly, mean spirited or committed. In this way we come to know something of ourselves and are able to grow and change. Spirit in this sense involves the basic orientation or disposition of our lives - it is that passion which animates or moves us.

This way of seeing spirit is similar to that set out by Plato. He refers to the 'spirited soul' as:

> That element in the person from which comes the dynamism for living. A person with 'spirit', a 'spirited person', is one who is 'alive': a person who is 'spiritless' is lacking in vital qualities and not fully alive'.[15]

In this sense spirit is about character - or at least some valued aspects. These include virtues like courage and indignation at injustice, as well as such qualities as being lively, energetic and full of life. This spirit is passionate. However, it isn't a slave of desires. It is influenced by reason. We can see this if we consider the virtues connected with it. They ask us to aim for goodness in all that we do. To know what this might mean we have to think matters through. Our desires and passions may push us in the direction of what might be good for us as individuals in the

---

[15] Rodger (1996), page 48. Plato discusses spirit, desires and reason as aspects of the soul or personality in *Republic*, paras.436b - 441c. For a discussion see Robin Waterfield's (1993) introduction to the Oxford University Press edition of the work.

short term; but our reason allows us to come to know what might be good for everyone.

The connection with virtues like courage indicates why there is talk of the 'leadership spirit' or 'spirit of leadership'. It might lead us in the direction of individuals - and to what motivates them to take on responsibilities and to seek to influence others. Equally, we can ask whether the process of leadership is conducted in the right spirit (with a respect for truth and the needs of others) or whether it is spirited (alive and vital).

Moral sense and conscience

As we have seen, acting in the right spirit entails being informed. But how does this come about? We have to work out what is right and wrong. This is a complex process involving feelings, values, attitudes, ideas and opinions. It is not usually a simple weighing up of clear-cut alternatives. Dilemmas abound. For example, walking down a road we find a £20 note. No one else is in sight. Do we pocket it - planning to top-up our electric meter? Do we hand it in at the local police station? Do we give it to charity or to someone we think is in need? In considering these we may find ourselves in dilemma. We are faced with a choice between alternative actions. Each alternative involves rights and wrongs, and there is no easy answer. If we add in our feelings and emotions the mix becomes more complex. We may have been brought up with the idea of 'finders keepers'; we may be poor with dependants; going into a police station might be a big hurdle because of previous experiences. So how do we decide what to do? This is where our moral sense or conscience comes into play.

Our conscience, according to Thomas Aquinas, is 'the mind of man making moral judgements'. This process involves us in drawing upon moral principles. These are guides to deliberation that have something to say about what is good and bad; right and wrong - about how people should behave. They are also the subjects of debate. While we may seek universal or broad agreement about them, they are always likely to be contested. The important thing is that we have a reasoned approach and can discuss that with others. Moral principles need reasons to justify them.

Feelings are not enough. Having some knowledge of those moral principles we can then relate them to the dilemma or question facing us. In this sense conscience is the seat of discernment, the space where we work out what to do. In the case of the £20 note we would have to consider how we feel as well what we think is right and wrong. We have to reflect on our wants and needs and compare them with those of others; what is just, fair and honest; and what is most likely to add to the sum of human happiness. We need to take into account previous experience and glean some truth from it (for example, one bad experience of a police station may not mean that our next encounter will be the same). Having deliberated we come to a decision and take some action.

The process does not stop here. Our actions have consequences. In reflecting on these we can learn. Keeping the £20 note may turn out to be a mistake. We might feel guilty, or later come to the conclusion that we have acted unjustly. Whatever, we learn. Our moral principles can come into question. We think about them critically. This may mean they are adjusted in the light of our experience. Our actions are evaluated and our position may shift as a result. This is a continual process of growth and change. Through it we can gain in wisdom.

If leadership is to have heart, then it must appeal to conscience and to moral principles. The process of discernment, of making good judgements, is both an individual and shared experience. As participants in the process of leadership we need to invite others to join with us in weighing up, and working out, alternative courses of action. Again this is complex. People will bring to the conversation different ideas about what is right and wrong. There are likely to be disagreements. It could have been members of a group that found the £20 note. Some may believe in 'finders keepers', whilst others might argue that it is not fair to the person who lost the money to keep it. These situations are often difficult to reconcile as people may be approaching the question from completely different mindsets. To move forward, we need to get beyond our individual consciences and moral principles and look to the group. We need to acknowledge difference and work towards gaining some common understanding. From this we may be able to develop a shared idea of what might make for the good. This can then help guide us in our deliberations and focus our actions. Even if we cannot come to an agreement, at least we have learnt. The dilemma has been talked about. Questions have been asked, comments challenged. We have thought about our own point of view and listened to the opinions of others. Problems have been faced up to and we have sought solutions. Through these conversations we can gain a different view of the world.

Bringing heart to situations involves the cultivation of wisdom, and the ability to work with others to make moral sense. As we saw earlier in Chapter 2, wisdom lies not so much in having fixed ideas, but in taking a position and then developing it as we experience situations. We need to be ready to recognize the limits of our knowledge and experience, and be able to admit our mistakes. All this needs framing within a developing and, hopefully, shared appreciation of good and evil, right and wrong.

If we think about this in terms of the classical models of leadership it is more likely that we would expect the leader to have wisdom, and to make choices and decisions. Here, the process of discernment focuses on the activities of one individual. To return to our example of the £20 note, the 'classical' leader of the group would have to work out what to do based largely on their own moral principles, feelings and experiences. They may well consult members, but it is their 'job' to come to a decision. Having done that, they may then have to convince the group of their chosen course of action. One outcome is that the consequences of any action taken would largely fall on the head of the leader. The process of discernment, of making good decisions, becomes an individual experience. A problem with this is, of course, that it lacks the vibrancy and possibilities of a wider debate. As a result, decisions taken may well be less wise.

The contrast with models of shared leadership is clear. Here it is the group that has to debate and decide what to do. They don't look to one person to have all the answers. Their concern is to work together to make wise decisions. The process of discernment becomes both an individual and a group activity. It requires as a starting point, some shared or common understanding of what constitutes right and wrong; good and evil; and the nature of justice. Equally it must entail a shared sense of responsibility for the actions taken by the group. The problem with all this is that decisions of this nature may be harder to come by and may not materialize. Things can also turn nasty; feelings can run high and disagreement is sometimes hard to bear. On the other hand, the benefit of this approach is that the process is enriched through the committed conversation of members: different viewpoints can be heard, people are included.

Being

Often when we talk about who we are, we describe what we do. We might say I am a teacher, a carpenter, or I am a mother. Taken on face value these seem more about the tasks we do and the roles we have. They are about being some*thing*. They are less about our being some*one*. Meister Eckhart suggests we need to approach things from a different angle: 'People should not consider so much what they are to do, as what they are'.[16] This means asking questions like, 'What kind of teacher or mother am I?' 'Am I compassionate, committed, loving...?' However, to find answers we have to turn to what we do. So our actions do matter. It is through our experiences that we become the people we are. And the people we are, is revealed through our actions.

As well as thinking about the relationship between being and doing, we also need to examine that of being and having. Erich Fromm talks about these as the two fundamental modes of existence. They describe how we relate to ourselves and to the world. Having is concerned with possessing and owning - with trying to make people and things our property. Being looks to the person we are. Consider, for example, students attending a lecture. How do they work with that experience? Do they listen to the lecturer, engage with the material and try to make sense of what they hear in relation to what they already know? In

[16] Meister Eckhart quoted in Erich Fromm (1978) *To Have or To Be?* London: Abacus, page 8.

contrast, do they try to memorize and note down word-for-word what the lecturer is saying?

> Students in the having mode must have but one aim: to hold on to what they have "learned", either by entrusting it firmly to their memories or by carefully guarding their notes. They do not have to produce or create something new.... The process of learning has an entirely different quality for students in the being mode... Instead of being passive receptacles of words and ideas, they listen, they *hear*, and most important, they *receive* and *respond* in an active, productive way.[17]

To engage with each other we need to *be* with one another. This isn't a matter of sitting back and 'letting it all happen'. Rather it is about connecting with each other. We sometimes hear people talk of being 'at peace with one another' or of being 'totally honest' with someone. These are hallmarks of *being with* others. It might involve conversation or silence. Whatever, it is an active process that isn't necessarily about activity. It is often difficult to describe, but known when experienced.

If we go back to our earlier discussions of leadership we can see that classical leadership is often more to do with having, and shared leadership with being. In the former, leadership is a role that is the property of one person. In addition, the leader has the answers to problems; gives direction and has vision, and possesses special qualities that set them apart from others. This makes it difficult for people to share in leadership. Even where they do, it often goes unrecognized because one person is named 'leader'. What is more, that person is more likely to act on others. Followers become possessions, for example, we might hear talk about 'my group' or 'my team'. In turn, the group or team is likely to be passive, allowing this to happen. They are also in having mode. They 'have' a leader who possesses knowledge.

---

[17] Erich Fromm (1979) *To Have or To Be?* London: Abacus, pages 37 - 38.

Shared leadership is more to do with being. People are interdependent; they are active participants in the process of leadership. It is less about people's position or role as to what goes on between them. All work and take responsibility for what goes on.

In conclusion

In this chapter we have been exploring some themes that are often spoken of, but rarely addressed in relation to leadership. Perhaps people are put off by the profound nature of the questions that have to be addressed. It may be that because these words pop up in everyday conversation, we assume common understandings and think that there is little more to be said. It is part of human experience to bring heart to what we do. Here we have tried to make a start on understanding what it might mean in relationship to leadership. However, this needs go further. Unless we build theory around our experiences, things can all too easily remain at the level of sentimental claptrap.

Follow up

There are several things you can do to follow up the exploration of leadership in this chapter.

Born and Bred? CD: Listen to Melissa Desbonnes talking about her experiences in *Role play* (track three) and consider her aspirations and situation and those of Nash Ali in *Camden United* (track two).

Born and Bred? web pages: Visit the heart page at www.infed.org/bornandbred. You'll find extra activities, further reading, and links to related pages.

Informal Education: conversation, democracy and learning. Read chapter six *Making difficult choices* and visit the support page at www.infed.org/foundations.

Chapter four

Leadership with heart

The way that I work is the way that I am with people.

I felt obligated in a really positive way... This place gave me so much I want to give it back. I didn't feel that I had to, but I wanted to, and I was determined to do that.

As we saw in chapter three, heart involves spirit, moral sense and being. These are about the kind of people we are, the things we are committed to, and the nature of our relationships with others. When linked to leadership these come out in three main ways:

- **Service** - undertaking tasks for the benefit of others.
- **Association** - people joining together in companionship or to organize.
- **Well-being** - concern for human flourishing and wholeness.

Service

Service, as an altruistic act of giving, is a rather unfashionable idea. We are much more likely to encounter it as part of a transaction. It is what we receive as customers or consumers. We buy it. Sometimes we are told to do it, for example, in the form of community service orders that the courts impose or as part of some employment creation programme that those without jobs are obliged to undertake. The act of giving becomes closely linked to paying. We 'pay' for our crimes or income support by 'giving' our labour. We can also see this happening in some of the programmes around volunteering. Many people undertake these with good intentions. However, for some, volunteering can become self-serving. It is less about serving others, than doing some activities that may advantage us. We develop skills, contacts and may even receive awards. There is nothing wrong with these things in themselves, but when they become the main purpose they undermine the heart of service (see *Exhibit 3*).

Exhibit 3: Choosing service over self-interest

Ultimately the choice we make is between service and self-interest. Both are attractive. The fire and intensity of self-interest seem to burn all around us. We search, so often in vain, to find leaders we can have faith in. Our doubts are not about our leaders' talents, but about their trustworthiness. We are unsure whether they are serving their institutions or themselves... We ourselves are no different. We are so career-minded, even though there are so few places to go. Or we have surrendered to life-style... We were born into the age of anxiety and have become adults in the age of self-interest.

The antidote to self-interest is to commit and to find cause. To commit to something outside of ourselves. To be part of creating something we care about so we can endure the sacrifice, risk and adventure that commitment entails. This is the deeper meaning of service.

Let the commitment and the cause be the place where we work... Our task is to create organizations we believe in and to do it as an offering, not a demand. No one will do it for us. Others have brought us this far. The next step is ours.

Peter Block (1993) *Stewardship. Choosing service over self-interest*, San Francisco: Berrett-Koehler, pages 9-10.

Service involves doing tasks for the benefit of others. For us it is an act of the heart. It is undertaken in the spirit of community, of being part of, and connected with, a larger whole. As members of society we receive from others - and may have a sense of general duty to reciprocate in some way. If we didn't we would be parasites. In serving we recognize our responsibilities to others. We also connect with something deep within us. As Matt Ridley has written, 'the human mind contains numerous instincts for building social co-operation'.[18] Service is an invitation, as Peter Block puts it, 'to commit and find cause' (see *Exhibit 3*).

The gift of service should not be taken lightly. Unfortunately both givers and receivers of service often run into trouble. The relationship is open to exploitation. Servers can become martyrs, either giving too much at the expense of their own happiness or revelling in their perceived sainthood. The act of giving attracts attention and some may wish to be over-indulged. This is not giving service; it is serving our own interests. The idea of getting something for nothing also seems attractive and many people are all too ready to take advantage of those who wish to serve. Too often those giving service are used and abused. They may suffer exhaustion or feel under-valued. In extreme cases they may be exploited to the point of mental breakdown. The relationship needs balance. Those involved in service, both givers and receivers need to look to the well-being of each and all. As with leadership, the act should be elevating. It should enhance well-being.

The idea of leadership as service has been around for some time. For example, it was common to hear politicians talking of themselves as 'servants of the electorate'. (Today they more likely to speak in self-interested terms about their 'career' in politics.) In management there was the idea of the 'servant leader'. One writer proclaimed that 'the great leader is seen as a servant first'.[19] Their first priority is to consider the needs of others, and to help to build the conditions for all to lead. Another approach is via the idea of stewardship. Stewardship is to hold something in trust. It is the willingness to be accountable for the well-being of the group or organization, 'by operating in service, rather than in

---

[18] Matt Ridley (1997) *The Origins of Virtue*, London: Penguin, page 262.

[19] Robert Greenleaf (1970) *The Servant as Leader*, Newton, Mass.: The Robert K. Greenleaf Center, page 2.

control, of those around us'.[20] According to Peter Block, we can tell when authentic service is experienced:

- There is a balance of power. People should be acting on their own choices.
- The primary commitment is to the larger community. Focussing too much attention on the individual or the small group breeds self-centredness.
- Each person joins in defining purpose and deciding on the culture and direction of the group or organization.
- There is a balanced and equitable distribution of rewards. Every member of the group or level of an organization should share in creating its wealth and expanding its resources. If it is successful, the benefits should be evenly shared.

Service in its authentic sense leads to, and is generated by, association.

Association

Voluntarily joining together in companionship or to undertake some task can bring both personal satisfaction and social benefit. Such association can also be a major educational force. It helps to create what Alexis de Tocqueville called some 150 years ago 'habits of the heart': mores that allow people to connect with each other and to identify with the wider community.[21] At an informal level association can be found in the daily activities of life. For example, we may see people joining together whilst walking

---

[20] Peter Block (1993) *Stewardship. Choosing service over self-interest*, San Francisco: Berrett-Koehler, pages x and xxi.

[21] See Robert N. Bellah *et al* (1996) *Habits of the Heart. Individualism and commitment in American life* 2e, Berkeley: University of California Press for a discussion of this in contemporary American life. Alexis de Tocqueville's (1994) *Democracy in America*, London: Fontana is still a very rewarding read. For 'habits of the heart' see pages 279 and 287.

their dogs in the park, or in organizing a shopping trip. More formally we may find association in community groups, clubs and societies.

The scale and scope of formal association is often not fully recognized. In Britain around 12 million women and men are currently involved in running some 1.3 million voluntary groups, teams and organizations. This is a huge number of people - over 25 per cent of the adult population. In addition, well over half the adult population belongs to a local voluntary organization.[22] It is sometimes said that people do not have the time they did for such involvement, and that there is a crisis in civic membership. Perhaps because of a growing individualism, and with the home becoming more of a centre for leisure, there are temptations to disengage from the larger society. Commitment to certain types of association has waned - for example, to political parties and some churches. But other associations, such as those involving mutual support, have grown.

There are also interesting movements in young people's involvement. The most common forms of belonging are to sports clubs and youth groups. The level of commitment to the former remains pretty constant over time, but involvement in adult-organized youth groups tails off sharply at about age 13-14. It is mostly replaced by more informal groupings of friends that organize activities for themselves. These might range from going out to see a film or to a club or pub, through to more complex things like going for a day trip or holiday.

Whether formal or informal, growing or declining, associations represent a formidable resource. Taking part in them can bring great satisfaction. It may be that they cater for a special interest, need or enthusiasm we have - like playing football or painting. They certainly can provide a

---

[22] These figures and for material on the educational role of associations see Konrad T. Elsdon with J. Reynolds and S. Stewart (1995) *Voluntary Organizations. Citizenship, learning and change*, Leicester: NIACE, page 47. For material on young people's participation see Malcolm Hill and Kay Tisdall (1997) *Children and Society*, Harlow: Longman.

place where we may meet, be with others, and make friends. Indeed, one of the main reasons that people join specialist clubs is less for the activity itself, than for the opportunities to meet and be with others. Associations, thus, have a strong social function; they can help provide a sense of belonging and identity. This applies to both formal and more informal associations.

Groups can be little democracies. Institutions such as churches, tenants groups and enthusiast clubs have structures and ways of working that should allow those involved a voice. In practice there are all sorts of problems around this - but the potential remains. They are places where people can have the experience of learning to live co-operatively. They are also part of larger political processes. Many were formed to represent people's interests, and are members of wider associations. For many of us local or small associations are the way in which we learn about, and participate in, politics. As Alex de Tocqueville wrote, 'Without local institutions a nation may give itself a free government, but it has not got the spirit of liberty.[23]

Associations also have great educational power. Through being involved in them people grow in confidence and self-belief. They are able to act in ways they had not expected. Much of this learning is unseen; for the most part it does not happen in formal educational sessions. As the landmark *1919 Report* on adult education saw, learning flows from 'the informal educations which come from sharing in a common life'.[24] In French there is a term for this experience of a common life - *la vie associative* (sometimes translated as the 'associative life'). Participation in the life of an association allows people to work together to achieve things. Becoming aware of why we join in and the processes involved is, in itself, a form of education.

The power of association has also been understood within youth work - but not made a priority in practice.

---

[23] de Toqueville (1994) page 63.

[24] Ministry of Reconstruction (1919) *Report of the Adult Education Committee of the Ministry of Reconstruction*, London: HMSO. Page 76.

Perhaps the best known example comes from way back in 1960. Then, the Albemarle Report famously declared that the primary aims of the youth service should be association, training and challenge. The Report had the following to say about association:

> To encourage young people to come together into groups of their own choosing is the fundamental task of the Service... (W)e want to call attention to:
>
> a) An opportunity for commitment.... Basically the group should provide ideals as well as activities and a warm and friendly atmosphere in which a young person can feel wanted and understood.
>
> b) An opportunity for counsel... Only too rarely do young people feel enough confidence in an older people and more experienced person to seek advice... We believe the good youth group should try to cater for these needs...
>
> c) An opportunity for self-determination... We value very highly the active participation of the young and their own leadership of groups which they bring into existence themselves. [25]

Sadly, this aspect of the Report was neglected. Instead services focused on provision *for* young people rather than *with* or *by* them. And that is the way that youth work has remained - in Britain and Ireland at least. Youth workers and youth services have mostly failed to grasp that fundamental task.

Given that association has been largely ignored it is little wonder that leadership has failed to capture the imagination of workers. It isn't simply that leadership is seen as 'old-fashioned' and elitist, taking it seriously would mean changing working practices. It is often much easier to put on

---

[25] Ministry of Education (1960) *The Youth Service in England and Wales* ('The Albemarle Report'), London: HMSO, pages 36 - 41 and 52 - 64.

activities and sessions for people rather than involving them in organizing. Working so that others develop groups and programmes can also feel very risky. Where there is pressure on workers to open centres and projects as often as they can, and to cater for larger numbers of people, a focus on association and self-determination seems to put all sorts of things out of their control.

Well-being

We have already argued that leadership should be inclusive - that all should share in the process and gain from it. In addition, we have said that it should be elevating - that we should become wiser and better people by being involved (see Chapter two). In other words, leadership should work so that people can flourish. But what does this actually mean?

The idea of flourishing is bound up with that of well-being, and with questions around the nature of human happiness and what sort of life is good to lead. Well-being, it can be said, is both what is needed for us to lead 'the good life' and what the good life accomplishes. To understand what this might mean we first have to draw a line between happiness as a good feeling or sense of euphoria, and happiness as flourishing or making a success of life. It is the latter, deeper, meaning that is important for us here. The ancient Greeks had a word for it- *eudaimonia* - and for philosophers like Aristotle it is the ultimate goal of life. This opens an obvious question; in what does flourishing consist? [26]

To flourish is to do things well. It is to have heart - to be animated by our passions, to engage with our moral senses and virtues, and to embrace life with other people in a fully human way. It is also, according to Aristotle, to be wise - to know about life, to contemplate and think, and to make good judgements (see chapter three). *Eudaemonia* means, literally, 'having a good guardian spirit'. However, well-

---

[26] This question is posed by Jonathan Barnes (1982) in *Aristotle*, Oxford: Oxford University Press, page 78.

being isn't only a personal and ethical matter; it is also political. People cannot flourish in situations where they are exploited and oppressed. They cannot flourish when they lack basic goods such as:

- The means of subsistence: adequate food, clothing, shelter and so on.
- Pleasure.
- Work, rest and play: these are the basic activities that people must engage in if their lives are to be well balanced, if they are to develop as human beings.
- Social relationships (being with friends, lovers and perhaps even rivals). [27]

There are likely to be endless debates about what we include in, and exclude from, a list like this. There will also be questions about the nature of the items, for example, what constitutes a good form of work and how much we should have of it. All this is not just of interest to philosophers. For example, educators might be considering them in relation to their activities. Parents are likely to be thinking about the sort of life they want for their children.

In many respects, what we have discussed as well-being comes very close to what we understand today as 'wholeness'. First, there is the linking of body, mind and spirit (or in Plato's terms - desire, reason and passion). Second, there is the connection of our selves with others. Third, these qualities are not just about connectedness to other people; they are also about the way we are with the world. To know something is to have a living relationship with it – to influence and be influenced by it. Another way of thinking about this is as being in communion with others and the world. We look to share and participate rather than dominate. Last, perhaps through such communion we may

---

[27] Alan Brown (1986) *Modern Political Philosophy. Theories of a just society*, Harmondsworth: Penguin, page 159. See, also, John Rawls (1972) *A Theory of Justice*, Oxford: Oxford University Press, for a discussion of primary goods (page 90 – 95).

connect with God or truth. We may feel a movement beyond our selves. This sense of transcendence, of being in touch with experiences that stand outside time and space, completes the circle. It is a feeling that can be deeply enriching as it flows through our lives.

Connection of this kind gives life a special meaning. We are part of something larger, something that is not constrained by the ordinary laws of physics and that we can never fully explain. It may well allow us to stand outside the hurly burly of our existence - if only for a moment - and sense how things fit together. This sense of knowing, which is often beyond words, seems to find its way through to the way in which we are in the world.

In conclusion

In this chapter we have been looking at how leadership with heart may be expressed. We have seen that it involves undertaking tasks for the benefit of others; a commitment to the life of groups; and a concern for the happiness of all. These ideas are pretty unfashionable, under-powered and often mutated within informal education and associated fields. Even where there is a concern, for example, for well-being, it can often get overshadowed or subverted by an emphasis on narrow objectives. Service, association and well-being must be embraced in their truest forms if we are to cultivate leadership with heart.

Follow up

There are several things you can do to follow up the exploration of leadership in this chapter.

Born and Bred? CD: Listen to Nash Ali talking about service, commitment and passion on *Camden United* (track two) and to the educators and participants involved in the Gateway Award project on *Garden Service* (track seven).

Born and Bred? web pages: Visit the leadership with heart page at www.infed.org/bornandbred. You'll find extra activities, further reading, and links to related pages.

Informal Education: conversation, democracy and learning. Read chapter three *Fostering democracy* and visit the support page at www.infed.org/foundations.

Part three

Informal education and leadership

In this part of the book we want to focus on the actions of informal educators and how they can stimulate the development of forms of leadership that allow all to flourish and grow.

Some of the ideas we turn to may be a little unfamiliar. In part this is because we have had to go back to some older, and almost forgotten, ways of making sense of informal education. Perhaps the most significant of these concerns the power of association, as we saw in Chapter 4. Here we also look at notions like character building. The relevance of these ideas has not lessened with time. Changing fashions have just obscured them - much as with leadership itself. We have also turned to some ideas that would be more familiar to continental European readers. Central among these are animation and formation. As we will see, such notions help us gain a deeper insight into the work of informal educators like youth workers, community development workers and community educators.

In Chapter five we explore the processes of animation, education and formation, and how the relate. We also look at their relevance for leadership. From there we go on, in Chapter six, to examine some of the key areas on which informal educators will have to focus if they are to develop leadership with heart.

Chapter five

Animation, education and formation

Because of the way I was treated and the way they talked to us, the way they delegated so much to us to do... we learned from that. That was something I was able to take back, and to realise what they are doing was appropriate and how they worked was appropriate. It taught me how to work appropriately.

The job of the informal educator involves animation, education and formation. Animation means, literally, to breathe life into some thing. Education (from *educere*) is to draw out, to lead forth; or to rear or bring up children or animals. Formation (from *formare*) in its simple dictionary sense means to mould, fashion by discipline or education (see *Exhibit 4*). Each of these brings out different qualities, as we shall see. However, it can be argued that each involves the others. Thus, informal educators like youth workers and community workers, who have a primary interest in promoting reflection and learning, will also look to stimulate and enliven situations (animation), and to work with people to fashion particular skills (formation). In this chapter we want to explore what this might mean in practice.

Animation

As workers we're there as 'catalysts'. I have a certain amount of resources, knowledge and skills, the young people

> *have a certain amount of resources, knowledge and skills, but between us we can create something where we can both learn from and explore who we are, what we are and why we are.*

Associated with chemical reactions, catalysts are agents of change. Seeing educators as such captures some of the essence of education. However, unlike their chemical counterparts educators also change. This aside, the idea of educators as catalysts, of them coming together with people to create situations where learning can happen has a long history. In France, Italy and a number of other European countries this process has often been described as 'animation'.

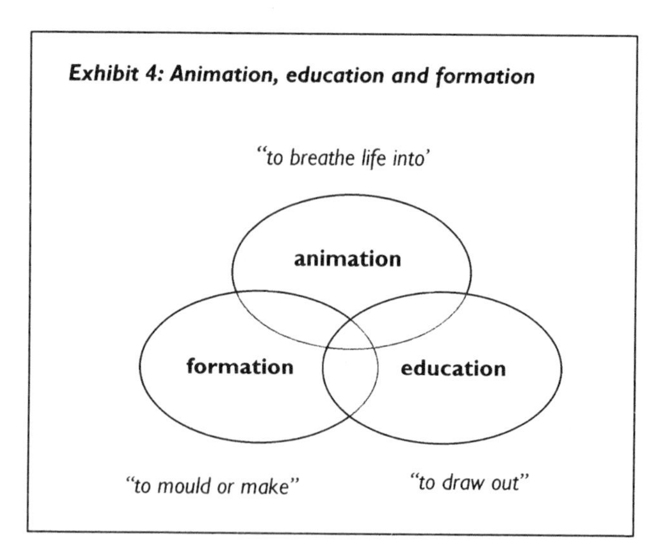

Animation is usually linked to the activities of informal educators like community workers, arts workers and youth workers. Examples include:

- Using theatre and play as means of self-expression with community groups, children and people with special learning needs (sometimes called creative-expressive animation). In Britain and Ireland this strand of animation is most often found in the activities of arts workers and therapists working in social education centres, clinics and rehabilitation centres.

- Working with people and groups so that they participate in and manage the communities in which they live (sometimes called socio-cultural animation). The closest link with British and Irish experience lies in the work of community development workers and community educators.
- Developing opportunities for pre-school and school-children such as adventure playgrounds, toy libraries, outdoor activity centres, and organized sports activities (sometimes called leisure-time animation and these days often run for profit). In Britain and Ireland, this has been a significant aspect of youth work and has recently taken a commercial turn in the form of play provision within workplaces, shopping malls and eateries.[28]

But what does animation involve? To animate is to transform. What was still now moves. In the English language animation is mostly associated with the work of filmmakers. Illustrators create action from a series of images and we have the sensation of something living. However, it is an illusion. The images pretend life. A line is drawn. There is a contrast between that which is alive and that which is inanimate: animals and plants are distinct from iron and rocks. The difference between them was for ancient Greeks like Aristotle, *psûché* (or *anima* in Latin) - soul, breath or life. In this sense then, animators work so that life may flow, movement may happen.

Animators (or animateurs) are sometimes seen as 'motivators'. The image we may have is of the trainer or fitness instructor pushing us to exercise, the holiday rep or 'redcoat' encouraging us to join in some activity. Many are not very happy with this. The emphasis on stimulation and inspiration can lead to animators trying to do things to people, rather than working with them. For example, we might be concerned with people who are out of work and

---

[28] The idea and practice of animation in Europe is explored by Walter Lorenz (1994) *Social Work in a Changing Europe*, London: Routledge.

who seem to lack the motivation to find a job or become involved in further education. The danger is that we try to act on them - pushing them into getting details of jobs, telling them they will feel better if they take care of their appearance, getting them up early in the morning. This tends to take responsibility away from them. We do things to them so that they act.

> *I honestly thought my role was to do things for the young people continuously... [But] how are they going to learn if we do it for them? I found that very difficult at the beginning.*

The problem is that motivation is not something that can be pushed into people - it develops through relationship and experience. Informal educators have to work to create the right environment. The people they are, and the situations that they help to make, are what count. Animators in this sense, look to breathe life into themselves and into situations rather than into other people.

There is something more about this interest in the social and situations. Deep worries about the withering away of social life were a key aspect of the turn to animation in France and Italy in the 1960s and 1970s. What was needed, it was argued, was a renewal or re-animation of communities. There were similar worries in Britain and Ireland at the same time. Alongside renewal came a focus on participation - of building more democratic ways of living. In other words, this strand of animation - like the ways of viewing leadership we discussed in Chapter two - carries within it a vision of the way life should be lived. Animators help to build environments and relationships in which all have a voice, can grow and have a care for each other.

Education

These ideas run quite close to the concerns of informal and experiential educators. Indeed, a recent book by David Boud and Nod Miller use the word 'animation' because of its connotations: to give life to, to quicken, to vivify, and to inspire. They widen out the term to mean 'acting with learners, or with others, in situations where learning is an aspect of what is occurring, to assist them to work with their experience'. [29] We can see that this view of animation is wider than what we have been focusing on (breathing life into situations). In fact it is very close to what we talk about as education generally.

We are constantly learning; developing new understandings. This can be as simple as coming to know how long it takes to boil an egg or as complex as appreciating our part in being treated badly by our brother. Often we learn without appearing to try. It just seems to happen. At other times we set out to learn something, for example, conversational French. We may even help others to learn. For example, we might teach our child a safe way to cross the road. In purposefully setting out to learn ourselves, or to help others learn, we are involved in education. Education involves intentionally fostering learning. However, there is more to it than this. We have to look to the values that inform the process. Education entails a commitment to certain ideals. These include a respect for persons, a commitment to work for truth, and an overarching concern for human well-being.

Decisions have to be made about what is learnt and how. Often these are taken out of the hands of the learner. For example, the National Curriculum sets out what is to be learnt by school children by certain key stages. Schools and teachers interpret this and determine the approach by which people will be taught. Learners are often viewed as empty vessels into which knowledge is poured.[30] Here knowledge is seen as the possession of certain individuals. It is administered and acquired; passed from one person to another. This can be a highly oppressive process.

It isn't only schools that adopt this approach. Often those working in health promotion or in crime reduction will have

---

[29] David Boud and Nod Miller (1997) *Working with experience. Animating learning*, London: Routledge, page 7.

[30] Carl Rogers' famously called this a 'jug and mug' theory of education. See 'The politics of education' in Howard Kirschenbaum and Valerie Land Henderson (eds.) (1990) *The Carl Rogers Reader*, London: Constable.

their own form of curriculum to follow. Much of this is about imposition. Content and method become something that learners have little say in. As such it is questionable as to whether these encounters constitute education. Rather the lack of choice means that they perhaps have more in common with indoctrination. Much of what goes on in schools, youth groups and community groups is, thus, indoctrination disguised as 'education'.

Educators act in ways that allow people to explore their experiences, attend to their feelings, and develop their understandings. They draw out rather than push in learning. Part of that action is to be around and approachable so that people can talk.

> *When I first started the post ... I found it hard sitting around having a chat, thinking 'Oh I'm getting paid for this' and I didn't really understand the importance of it until further on into my role. Conversation plays a big part in our jobs.*

When looking at what informal educators do, it is easy to be misled by appearances. They may organize various activities, but as educators their primary interest lies in helping people to create an environment in which they can reflect and learn. That process involves a lot of talking and listening. Conversation lies at the heart of their work. Much of the time conversations will be about everyday things. Here informal educators will simply go with the flow-valuing the relationships and feelings that are built through such talk. At other times they will be making their contribution in order to draw out learning. From the outside it may just seem like a group of people chatting. From the inside it is a very sophisticated form of education.

As well as drawing out learning, educators work with people to create situations that open up new possibilities. In other words, they animate. For example, they may encourage a group to try something they have not done before. It could be anything from reading bits of *The Guardian* to walking on the hills. We know that the stimulation of new experiences can lead to exploring different aspects of our lives, as well as being interesting and enjoyable in themselves. Breathing life into situations involves both being around in them, and creating new opportunities.

Formation

To complete our introduction we need to look at the ways that thinking around training has developed in Europe. Formation, as we have seen, means to mould; fashion by discipline or education. It is sometimes translated as 'training'. It might be applied to gaining the sort of skills involved in driving a car, or to developing the abilities needed to do a particular job. Informal educators are often engaged in this sort of formation. They work to develop people's skills in specific areas. What is of special interest here is that people are engaging with them through choice. If training is happening it should be because people want it. Talk of 'moulding and making' can make it seem like the educator acts on other people - making them into this or that. In the open relationships of informal education both educators and those they are working with participate. They work together to develop skills.

However, informal educators are also familiar with formation in a rather different guise. For many it has been the central concern of youth work. Better known as 'character-building' or 'character training', formation has been a consistent part of scouting, boys clubs and adventure education. In Britain the efforts of teachers and heads in the public schools in the mid-nineteenth century did much to bring character-building to the fore. The concern was to develop people's (largely young men's) abilities to act 'for the best' when called upon. They had to 'Be Prepared' as Robert Baden-Powell's famous motto put it. Traditionally, character builders emphasized physical exercise, self-discipline, service to others, leadership and development of individual interests. Character was the balanced development of individual powers. It meant attending to body, mind and spirit. Just as muscles could be toned through exercise, so character could be trained.

Today the language of character building seems dated and quaint. But the idea lives on. Many youth workers, for example, still seem to want to shape behaviour and beliefs. This intention is clothed in a different language and so is difficult to see at times. A good example of this is the way in which smoking is approached. The talk may be of 'educating for health' or 'promoting healthy options' but there are some very strong messages involved. No smoking rules in youth and community buildings, workers acting as 'good role models' and not smoking themselves while on duty, and frequent inputs on the dangers of the 'habit' are common. The attitude adopted can range from the downright condemnatory to the more exploratory. Sadly, some workers may try to impose behaviours on young people rather than to work with them. This has not been helped by the anxiety of agencies to show that they are 'doing something' about particular issues and to meet the narrow demands of funders. However, many of the same themes appear, for example, an emphasis on self-restraint, a stressing of the impact of their behaviour on others, and the creating of a disciplined environment. In this way the overall experience for many young people is close to that of character building.

It needn't be this way. Formation can be something that is shared between informal educators and those they work with. Together they can be looking to build skills. Together they can be working to deepen capacities.

Animation, education and formation

There are great areas of overlap in these three approaches, for example the way that each could be seen to have a concern with 'being' (see chapter three). However, they do bring out different dimensions. There are times when workers seek to open up possibilities and to encourage people to become involved in some activity, experience or campaign. At other times they will seek to create an environment in which people can develop specific skills (and hopefully, also to link them to some wider purpose and meaning). There will also be times when workers encourage people to reflect on their feelings, experiences and ideas.

Each could be said to have an active and a passive side. The passive side is often associated with treating people like objects. Workers breathe life into them; they try to shape them. They act on them. An 'active' orientation views people as subjects, as active agents. Here workers are concerned with the environment and interaction. They look to people as participants. They join with them in their struggles to make sense of themselves and the world - and to act.

In some countries, animation has become the work of youth workers, community development workers and informal educators generally; formation the task of trainers – social, vocational and professional; and education is associated with teachers in schools and colleges. In other words, people have become defined by the sort of agency they work in. We see this as a crude and unhelpful division. Rather than look at the agency we need to look at what people actually do, and the ideas and values that guide their actions. Whether we name people trainers, educators or animators should depend on the emphasis in their work. If their main concern is with learning and reflection then we may describe them as educators. Where the primary focus is on enlivening situations we can name them animators (even though their work may involve formation and education). Similarly, those mostly concerned with training would be called formators.

In conclusion

From what has been said so far, we can draw a number of conclusions. We want to focus on three.

First, it could be said that leadership involves animation, education and formation. As we saw in Chapter two, writers like Ronald A. Heifetz have already argued that it entails educating.

> 'Leadership is a special sort of educating in which the teacher raises problems, questions, options, interpretations, and perspectives, often without answers, gauging all the while when to push through and when to hold steady.'[31]

However, stimulation is also necessary if people are to face up to their responsibilities, and play their part (animation). There will also need to be a focus on coaching or the development of particular skills (formation).

---

[31] Ronald A. Heifetz (1994) page 245.

Second, if true leaders are educators, are educators leaders? The simple answer is that they can be. As we saw in part one, leadership can be viewed in very different ways. In classical leadership models, the educator may be seen as the named leader and would embrace all that entails. Given that the process of education requires sharing responsibility, whether this would be a wise move for an educator is debatable. Within shared leadership models all may lead - educators included.

Third, educators need to pay more attention to animation. As we have seen, while reflection and the nurturing of specific skills play vital roles in the opening up of leadership, stimulation - the process of enlivening - is an area of great significance. This has been long recognized by those seeking to develop 'leadership skills' - especially in adventure education. However, little thought has been given to the nature of that animation and its relation to education and formation - at least within English-language traditions. By looking to situations, having a concern for life and flow, and placing these within a commitment to the happiness of all, educators deepen their practice.

Follow up

There are several things you can do to follow up the exploration of leadership in this chapter.

Born and Bred? CD: Listen to the workers at the Ladder Project talk about their experiences of developing as educators on *Time and talent* (track 4).

Born and Bred? web pages: Visit the animation page linked to the book at www.infed.org/bornandbred. You'll find extra activities, further reading, and links to related pages.

Informal Education: conversation, democracy and learning. Read chapters one (*Being an informal educator*), two (*Trusting in conversation*) and three (*Fostering democracy*). Visit the support page at www.infed.org/foundations.

Chapter six

Cultivating leadership with heart

> *There was no real discussion, no real democracy and so they started leaving. He said to me 'Why are they leaving? Why won't they do what I want them to do?' I said about ownership and about dictators and... yes, democracy does take a long time because you have got to get people to agree, but it is important because then they all have ownership, they are not following a leader, they are being part of the whole process.*

When educators do talk of developing leadership, the next step is usually a move to activity. People are set some challenge or problem to solve - and are left to get on with it. After the allotted time, they are brought together with the educators - and the experience is explored. Often challenges are manufactured; they are exercises or simulations. As useful and enjoyable as this may be, we think this largely misses the point. Special activities have their place, but it is the everyday experience of leadership that requires particular attention. We need to be thinking about the way in which we can open up the power of association. To animate and develop leadership we need to attend to association and to ideals of service. We must explore how we can foster creative participation. The main tool informal educators have is the way they are with people. How they answer people's questions, whether they value their company, what they expect from them - these are the sort of things that matter.

There is often talk of being a role model; a good example of the kind of person we should all be. It is important to act with integrity and people may learn through being with us. However, it can be dangerous to accept, or put ourselves up as, models of ideal citizens. First, we are not perfect so it is only a matter of time before our flaws are identified. Second, being seen as 'perfect' by others may lead to us being unapproachable. Further, it places undue pressure on us to perform at all times. Third, it can allow us to sit on our laurels - why would we need to develop and grow if we were already perfect? Fourth, it encourages mimicry in others. If we are perceived as a role model it follows that others may try to be like us. This can undermine their potential to develop as unique individuals.

Here we have picked some important areas to think about. To develop environments where people can take responsibility and have a concern for each other, educators must:

- Aim for democracy.
- Commit to mutual aid.
- Work for a clear focus.
- Attend to people's feelings.
- Encourage positive interaction.
- Develop structures.
- Know the place of special activities.
- Attend to reflection and learning.

For many informal educators these are 'bread and butter' concerns. They should be central to what they do.

Aim for democracy

Informal educators have to respond in very different situations. At one moment they may be working with someone who is distraught following the death of a parent, at another trying to deal with an argument over who is next on the pool table. For a lot of the time they have little say in the issues that face them. These come from those being worked with. This is one of the special features of informal education. Yet while immediate aims may change from situation to situation, the fundamental purpose remains the same. Educators should be working so that all may share in a common life. This involves many of the qualities we have been exploring with regard to the spirit of leadership. It includes animating situations where people can develop:

- Mutual respect and a concern for others' needs.
- Readiness to take and share responsibility.
- Commitment to conversation and to community.
- Knowledge of the issues and situations facing them.
- Particular skills.

In other words, educators share a larger purpose, namely to foster democracy.

Informal educators always need to be asking the larger question. It would be very easy to get submerged under the various issues that people bring up, or under the sometimes ill informed demands of the agencies they may work for. To get funding, agencies often have to chase the latest moral panic - drugs, lone parents, school non-attendance, whatever. This then translates into demands that workers do something about the chosen issue, and their work is assessed around this. All the time they need to be asking simple questions like: 'How does what I am doing now contribute to people being able to share in a common life?' 'In what ways can I work for democracy?'

Commit to mutual aid

As we have already seen, informal educators are concerned with people's participation in conversation. They look for co-operation, for people joining in and to whether there is thought of others' feelings and openness to what they say. However, informal educators need to move beyond this into involvement in making decisions and taking responsibility. They need to shift from situations where group members view organization as being done by 'one of them, for us' to where (at least) it is done 'by some of us, for all of us'.[32] This is getting toward what the writers of the Albemarle Report meant by the active participation of people: 'their own leadership of groups which they bring into existence themselves' (see chapter four).

It is one thing having aims, quite another to have the motivation and commitment to carry them through. Workers have to want to pick up, and create, all the opportunities they can to animate concern between people, and encourage them to take responsibility for their lives, learning and the situations they encounter. Part of the resistance to taking this step can come from not being able, or knowing when, to hold back.

> *What I found was that I was having to hold back an incredible amount because I'd just want to get involved, so it would be quick and easy. But I didn't. I pulled right back because the experience would have been different for the group.*

Workers may have little experience of working in this way, and little idea of how things will work out.

For those interested in working so that people take responsibility for their groups and activities, it is worth bearing in mind the following as starters.

- It usually takes time to build up a tradition of working in this way. People have to get used to workers putting things back to them: 'What do you want to do?' 'How are you going to organize that?'
- Informal educators need handy explanations for what they are doing, such as: 'I'm not here to take over. Perhaps we can work together on this'.
- It is important to be on the look out for people and situations that can be developed. As one worker put it:

---

[32] This phrase is taken from the excellent review of mutual aid in leisure undertaken by Jeff Bishop and Paul Hoggett (1986) *Organizing Around Enthusiasms. Mutual aid in leisure*, London: Comedia.

> *If I can see that someone has a talent or skill, then I'll suggest things to them and perhaps get them to explore that area. If I can see someone who has a talent or skill in organising or a manner in which people will listen to them then I'd encourage them to take on a coordinatory role.*

- Many educators find it best to start with encouraging people to undertake smaller, manageable activities - like organizing a session or an outing. Having learned and gained confidence from that they can move on to more ambitious projects. The same applies to educators!

Much of the work will take the form of 'hatching and despatching'. The task is to pick up on people's interests and to help them to animate, and organize around, these. Once they have gained those abilities, or organized the thing they wanted, educators may not see them again. In other words, they may end up working with some groups for quite short, but intensive, periods of time. Where the projects that people want to do are more ambitious, or where people are less confident or focused (see below), then long-term work may be required.

What we are suggesting here is that when working with groups two emphases are required: to animate and develop democratic mutual aid, and to work with the group so that it achieves its purposes.

Work for a clear focus

One of the lessons we can draw from studies of groups where people take responsibility and share in decisions is that they have focus. In other words, the purpose of the group is clear. Perhaps the most common examples of such groups are those organized around an interest like making music and playing sport. These mutual aid groups bring people together who have an enthusiasm and want to take it further. That focus attracts others with similar interests. People often want the chance to meet and make friends with those of like mind. They may also want to gain information, training and resources around their interests; and to take part in collective rather than individual projects. For some groups the focus is clear, others might want help to nail down the exact nature of their interest. It could be that they cannot put into words what they want, or that their focus needs narrowing into something more manageable.

An advantage of groups with a sharp focus is that it is likely that people will have clear expectations about what they will get from membership, and what they may have to contribute. The fact that members are interested and enthusiastic about a thing means that they are more likely to be motivated and committed to do something. They are also more likely to act with each other. Having a shared focus means that there is the possibility of achieving at least part of what they want. These factors can provide a push start to a group that is keen on organizing things for itself. They can also sustain it through hard times.

A lot of the groups informal educators come across do not have such an obvious focus. They are not built around an overt enthusiasm. However, they do have purpose - otherwise they would not exist. If we think about groups of friends, for example, we can see that they take part in activities. They do various things. These may involve meeting up for a drink, and helping each other out with practical tasks like moving home or sharing childcare. Sometimes the activity catches our attention. However, like the mutual aid activities we discussed above, a group's main reason for being often lies elsewhere. People want company and friendship. When working with such groups our task is, thus, on the one hand, to work for democratic mutual aid. [33] On the other hand, it is to help people to animate and realize their purpose - in this case to have satisfying social relationships.

The two tasks are connected. Educators may well be exploring the quality of relationships with members of the group in different ways. They may be looking to animate situations where people treat each other with respect or involve each other in making decisions. At the same time

---

[33] This way of looking at working with groups can be explored in Urania Glassman and Len Kates (1990) *Group Work. A humanistic approach*, Newbury Park: Sage.

they are likely to be asking people to reflect on the reasons why they spend time together. Informal educators can work so that groups are satisfying to their members – and being clear about focus helps.

Attend to people's feelings

As Ronald A. Heifetz has noted, we need to recognize that change involves stress and that without stress it is unlikely that real change will happen.[34] When fostering leadership, three main areas seem to create stress for participants. First, there are personal anxieties around the process of taking responsibility: 'Am I up to this?' 'What happens if things go wrong?' 'What will the others think of me?' Second, there are often tensions within groups as members consider what each other are doing. There may be feelings of jealousy, or a fear, of a particular person 'getting too big for her boots' and so on. Third, there can be stresses arising out of the focus for activity. The issue or problem that the group is trying to address may cause anxiety in itself – fundraising in order to stop a club being closed down; organizing so that a member of the group has the space to mourn the death of someone close.

In these situations educators need to work to contain stress and to keep it within tolerable limits. Heifetz has described this process as creating a holding environment. As we mentioned earlier, it involves animating and fostering relationships that allow people to feel safe enough to think about things and to act. The term 'holding environment' came originally from psychoanalysis.

> The therapist "holds" the patient in a process of developmental learning in a way that has some similarities to the way a mother and father hold their newborn and maturing children. For a child the holding environment serves as a containing vessel for

---

34 Ronald A. Heifetz (1994) *Leadership Without Easy Answers*, Cambridge, Ma.: Belknap Press, pages 104 –113. The later quote is taken from page 104.

> the developmental steps, problems, crises, and stresses of growing up.

Educators have to work so that people feel similarly protected. Within the space created, they can begin to examine the anxieties and problems facing them and to make some progress in addressing them. When people feel they are in a 'safe pair of hands', they can perhaps begin to think more clearly about an issue. Thus, part of the process involves educators in showing that they have some understanding and sympathy for the situation facing people. It also involves inviting people to look at what is going on when the moment is right. However, the danger is that they become over-reliant on educators or particular leaders and the holding environment becomes a special kind of prison. It is so safe that there is no particular desire to escape it.

Crucially, creating a holding environment is an ability that educators both need to develop in themselves, and to encourage in others. As Heifetz shows, creating holding environments is an important aspect of leadership. Thus, in working with groups, it is often necessary to explore how people can act together to contain situations and develop ways in which they can make it safe for themselves (and others) to deal with difficult issues.

So far we have tended to look at one side of things. Feelings can both get in the way and animate us. At times we can be so emotionally bound up in a situation that we cannot see the wood for the trees. Equally, we can be motivated to act by our love for someone, or by a sense of fulfilment. It is important to check feelings, making sure the actions that flow from them are healthy for others and ourselves. Feelings can also give clues about situations that simple logic does not reveal. We may have 'gut feelings' about something. Attending to these, asking ourselves from where impressions may have come, can lead to new understandings. It is important not to ignore or view them negatively. They are part of our humanness. Being in touch with feelings, and showing them appropriately when the time is right, allows educators to meet with people as human beings.

Encourage positive interaction

As we have already seen in our exploration of shared leadership, educators need to be working so that people are able to talk with each other about their experiences. Conversation is important both because it allows for issues to be explored and news to be shared, and because it involves and strengthens many of the qualities that are required so that we may all lead fulfilling lives. To talk and listen we need to have a concern for other people, trust them and respect them. Here we want to highlight some key themes that we have found most helpful when working as educators.

- Conversation is not about trying to win an argument. It is about deepening understanding. This does not mean that educators should avoid challenge and debate - but they need to be aware of the spirit in which they take part.
- Conversation involves listening as well as talking - and to do both we need to think about other people's feelings and experiences. We need to give each other space to talk and to listen.
- Conversation involves a shared topic. A lot of the time people talk past each other. They fail to share a topic. In reality many conversations are more like monologues - with each person developing an individual point rather than coming together to explore what is between them.
- Conversation is unpredictable. It involves us in 'going with the flow'. Rather than us leading it, the material often leads us. This is part of its magic. We can find ourselves in unexpected places with new insights. However, we can also end well off-track. Often this doesn't matter, but there will be times when educators need to intervene to try to bring back the focus. This is an area where they need to take great care not to hijack the conversation.
- Conversations change. Sometimes they are simply chats - perhaps about television or the weather. At other times they will be much more formal - perhaps where someone wants to talk about a personal problem. For informal

> educators this can involve great skill. Often chats can quickly shift into something more serious, and back out again. They have to be able to change gear, and perhaps suggest a different setting to talk, for example, 'Shall we take a walk?'[35]

Informal educators should look to animate and foster creative participation; and encourage people to work together in ways that can bring out the best in themselves, others and situations. Working so that people can fully engage in conversation is a crucial aspect of that task.

Develop structures

If people are to participate in making decisions structure is needed for their activities. Some rules are required if things are to be fair and open. These might cover how decisions are made, who has to be present, the aim of the group, how money is to be handled, and so on. The main formal way of doing this with groups is by means of a constitution. Informally it is done through conversation and verbal agreement (sometimes with the addition of someone keeping notes). Without rules of some kind, there can be all sorts of problems. These can range from chaotic meetings, through money disappearing, to individuals making decisions on their own for the group.

We can often make too much of formal structures. While informal educators do need to build them or open them up in some situations (more of this later), a great deal can be done through encouraging people to create more informal forms of association. Within youth work, for example, there is a tendency to draw suggestions for activities into the agency. For example, a group of young people may want to go on a trip to Alton Towers. The classic response of workers is to sound out others in the project or centre – and then to

---

[35] Tony Jeffs and Mark K. Smith develop these points in (1999) *Informal Education: conversation, democracy and learning*, Ticknall: Education Now. Deborah Tannen has also written a number of books that help us to explore everyday conversation. See, for example, (1992) *That's Not What I Mean!*, London: Virago.

organize the trip - possibly involving some of those who made the original suggestion. An alternative route that the educator can take is to work with the group to organize something themselves. This may well mean encouraging them to look round at local coach companies to see what excursions they are organizing; to see what outings may be possible by train; or to explore who might drive them (e.g. an older sister or parent). It's then down to the group to carry the activity through.

Often within youth work, again, educators place great store in creating ground-rules with groups. At times these turn into 'contracts' that participants are expected to sign or at least agree to verbally. When such rules are broken sanctions are imposed. On the face of it these actions seem fair, however they tend to cut down opportunities for discussion. Groups may learn more from dealing with issues as and when they arise rather than trying to manufacture procedures for every eventuality. The extent to which these rules become binding and non-negotiable is questionable. Educators should look for opportunities to discuss behaviour within groups rather than to condone or condemn; punish or reward.

With a bit of foresight on the part of the educator and the agency, some more formal responses may be possible. If the agency sees itself as working with people to take responsibility - and has grasped the idea of association - then it could organize itself more on the model of a development agency. The task of the agency is then to help to animate situations where people form groups and do things for themselves. For example, in the case of the trip, the worker may well have access to a key resource like a minibus. Rather than put on the trip, they could be in the position to say 'You organize things, get the necessary permissions etc. and hire us to drive you there and to provide any necessary supervision and support'. In other words, the group can 'contract' the agency to do the work they may be unable to fund or undertake for legal reasons (like hiring and driving the bus). A similar approach could be taken around other interests and enthusiasms. The agency may well have access to rooms and spaces that it can 'hire out' to groups along with the appropriate support for them to put on activities.

A more ambitious approach is not just to develop people's ability to organize, but also to build more formal groups and organizations. This is a long-term activity - and may not be relevant for many groups. People's interests change, friends fall out or drift apart, and activities may only be needed to fill a gap. The scale of work involved in setting up and maintaining a formal group can be quite daunting - especially when it grows, takes on premises and employs workers (as is the case of the Magnet Centre and Tangents on the *Born and Bred?* CD). It involves animating situations where there are special kinds of relationship.

> *Everyone is equal, the member of staff, or a user, or a member on the committee... It just means that some people have more responsibilities than others and have to do a bit of decision-making.*

However, many groups do not need to develop on this scale. It might be that they could use the resources of an umbrella body like a church, youth centre or community association. Perhaps the main challenge here is to create environments and structures within such agencies so new groups can access them.

Know the place of special activity

So far we have concentrated on informal educators developing leadership and association largely through day to day conversation and involvement in organizing. We see this as central: people learning by doing.

> *They are picking up stuff; they are developing confidence, because none of them do it the same... They are developing their own skills in how to handle different situations. I don't think it is about writing down, you know this is how, if this situation arises that's the answer to it. I don't think any of it is about that, I think it's about giving them the opportunities to experience different situations, see how the people cope with that and then to get them to question.*

However, such work cannot stand-alone. It generally needs to be augmented by special activities such as training events or debriefing sessions.

> *We get them to question whether they could do it that way, or whether they need to think of a different way. As they continue to do this, take on that role, they then start taking on more responsibility of the leadership on board as they become more confident.*

People need space to reflect and learn. Often workers rely on activities that take people out of their everyday settings to achieve this. This approach, though useful in some cases, has problems:

> *One of the difficulties of working with people out of their day-to-day environment is making sense of the experience that they are having - what sense does it have when they are on the back streets of their hometown? What is the link?*

This has been one of the big issues around the leadership development activities associated with Outward Bound and other adventure programmes. However, the significance of things like residential training events - especially where it involves outdoor activities and simulations - is not so much what people learn directly about leadership or taking responsibility, but the fact that it is out of the ordinary. It is something different that people can enjoy (or endure) and reflect upon. The experience of being away, out of the normal run of things, may well give people space to think about their lives. They may meet people or situations that they come to identify with - and this can become a major animating force. There is not likely to be a direct transfer of learning from such settings to the daily lives of those involved. However, there may be some important shifts in disposition - the way we experience the world (see chapter three).

To things like residentials can be added more modest events and sessions that focus on specific skills or on gaining understanding about some particular aspect of organizing. Sometimes sessions are put together into courses around things like community involvement, but for the most part their utility lies in being organized when people need them. It may take various forms. For example, it could involve individual coaching such as when working with a 'treasurer' to develop their book-keeping skills; activities in meetings or committees around a specific area such as agenda-making;

or special briefing sessions around an issue (like the impact of new legislation on volunteering).

Attend to reflection and learning

One of the critical features here is the emphasis given to reflection by participants and educators.

> *To be able to reflect on processes and recognise the skills that people have got, as opposed to the skills that they haven't, and to recognise the importance of that. People don't always see what they've done well.*

It is all too easy to focus on task. Organizing an event or dealing with a problem can quickly sideline attention to process and the learning involved. The pressure to get things done can push out education. Even where educators set up special activities to stimulate learning, reflection can get missed. Educators can fall into the trap of thinking that the simple experience of an exercise or activity is enough. It usually isn't. People need to recapture experience and develop some understanding of it. In other words, we need to reflect on the situations we have encountered. This involves:

- **Returning to experiences** - recalling events and situations.
- **Attending to (and connecting with) feelings** - the 'good' and the 'bad'.
- **Evaluating experience** - thinking about experiences in the light of intentions, values, knowledge and skills, and then building some understandings about this.[36]

Just how informal educators do this with individuals and groups varies from situation to situation. In more formal

---

[36] This model is taken from the work of David Boud and associates. See the chapter on reflection in Tony Jeffs and Mark K. Smith (1999) *Informal Education: conversation, democracy and learning*, Ticknall: Education Now.

situations, perhaps on a training programme, it is possible to use a range of things - as does the following educator.

> *We have one-to-one evaluations, group evaluations and a self-assessment form they fill out. Things like how they feel they're getting on, what they've learnt, problems or dilemmas, how they've worked with others, It's about where they're coming from as opposed to where I feel they're coming from.*

Encouraging people to reflect in more informal situations involves educators in various strategies. Often it simply means that they introduce the subject of feelings, or what people made of different experiences into conversations. At other times they may try to create special spaces for reflection. Perhaps one of the most common techniques is to encourage groups to put aside some time at the end of a meeting or session to evaluate what has gone on. This may focus both on individual learning, and on how the group may work better.

> *Evaluation is done in a number of different ways. It's quite a balanced review because they say what they think they could've [been] improved on, but they also say what they thought was good. They look at ways of maybe trying to improve that for each other and learning from each other... There's that whole dynamic happening that they're learning off each other whilst trying to discover what they're like in those roles.*

In conclusion

In this chapter we have looked at some of the things that educators need to have at the top of their agenda when addressing leadership and to be true to the heart of their practice. As animators they seek to bring things to life. As educators they should seek to draw out, and to develop, learning. They also need to look to how leadership is born and bred and how they might enhance this process.

Follow up

There are several things you can do to follow up the exploration of leadership in this chapter.

Born and Bred? CD: Listen to workers and participants talking about their experiences of a residential event on *Building teepees* (track six); and to Nash Ali talking about team / association on *Camden United* (track two).

Born and Bred? web pages: Visit the cultivating leadership page at www.infed.org/bornandbred. You'll find extra activities, further reading, and links to related pages.

Informal Education: conversation, democracy and learning. Read chapters two (*Trusting in conversation*), three (*Fostering democracy*) and four (*Exploring reflection and learning*). Visit the support page at www.infed.org/foundations.

Conclusion

In this book we have argued that informal educators are uniquely placed to cultivate leadership with heart. Their emphasis on conversation and democratic practice, combined with the nature of the organizations and groups they work with, and in, opens up rich possibilities. However, there has to be some question as to whether they grab this opportunity. In this conclusion we want to outline some of the key problems.

First, many of those we may label as informal educators such as youth workers and community workers do not fully understand themselves as educators. Few professional training programmes pay proper attention to educational theory and practice, and there is only a rudimentary understanding of it in the field. An example of this has been the adoption of curriculum thinking in youth work policy making and management. This has given the appearance of agencies embracing an educational methodology, but in reality has demonstrated a fundamental misunderstanding of the process of informal education. It, by definition, is conversation- rather curriculum-based. As we commented in chapter five, many of the approaches adopted have been clothed in progressive language, but are actually deeply controlling and come close to indoctrination. Lack of attention to educational theory and practice, combined with parochialism and a more general failure to value theorizing has contributed to a lack of sophistication in the work. Insights and ideas from other cultures and traditions, such as animation, have not been exploited to their full potential.

Second, there has been a tendency among some youth workers, community workers and community adult educators to build their professional identity around a resistance to the 'mainstream'. They define themselves by what they are not: social workers and, in particular, teachers. However, they often have difficulty in saying what they are. Thus, in an attempt to portray themselves as being outside the 'system', many workers shy away from what may be seen as traditional ideas such as leadership. In so doing they fail to address some basic human experiences. Ironically, such radical or alternative posturing actually becomes deeply conservative. By leaving key notions like leadership unexplored, they make their own contribution to maintaining the status quo.

Third, as our comments in chapter four regarding association indicate, there has been a failure to face up to the fundamental task of youth work. There have been similar failures in community adult education. For example, the current concern with lifelong learning has been approached largely as an individual experience. The interest appears to lie primarily in opening up opportunities for individuals to gain skills and qualifications that may help with their careers and, more generally, further economic growth. Community work has also displayed an economic turn. This is not to say that these matters are unimportant, but it is to recognize that there has been a general shift away from association and group life. This is a particular worry given our focus here on cultivating leadership with heart.

Part of the responsibility for this failure lies in the hands of government. The perceived need to control social expenditure and to direct and target resources has led to a crude emphasis on issues-based practice with pre-determined outcomes. Work that takes time or that is hard to measure (such as that concerned with human flourishing) tends to be rejected in favour of the short-term payoff. However, workers have often played their part. To hold onto funding they have tailored their practice to meet narrow objectives that are often skill- or competency-based. Ticking boxes can be satisfying - and certainly reduces the need to think! Some workers may well be playing the system here - by presenting their work to funders in a palatable form whilst holding on to a concern for process rather than product. This is a dangerous game to play. It can start to become easier to go with the demands of funders and policymakers. This has the overall effect of making practice less adventurous and often crude. It does nothing to further understanding of an often misunderstood field. The heart is taken out of the work, and educators become jaded. Constantly having to make the case for conversation and democratic process to people that want to hear that something concrete has been 'done' about some social problem or moral panic can be exhausting. Team this with a lack of understanding of informal education by workers and managers, and the mix becomes catastrophic.

These problems highlight the plight of those educators and agencies that struggle to work for service, association and well-being. However, as some of the examples in this book and the associated CD demonstrate, there are those who take a different path. They attempt to work with the difficulties that face them. They take on ideas like leadership and work them into existing understandings of practice. This process relies on courage, a willingness to learn, a level of knowledge about themselves and their field, and the ability to translate this into practical action. It requires heart.